How Fifteen Transnational Corporations Manage Public Affairs

S. Watson Dunn
Dean, College of Business and Public Administration
University of Missouri, Columbia

with

Martin F. Cahill
President, The Public Policy Group
Lafayette, New Jersey

and

Jean J. Boddewyn
Professor of International Business
Baruch School, City University of New York

A University of Illinois surve
of international business prac
conducted under a
Marsteller Foundation grant

Crain Books
Crain Communications Inc.
740 Rush Street
Chicago, Illinois 60611

Library of Congress Classification: LC 79-52256
International Standard Book Number: ISBN 0-87251-039-5

Printed in the United States of America.
Design and typesetting: North Coast Associates.

769

1000677151

How Fifteen Transnational Corporations Manage Public Affairs

Contents

Foreword

During the past decade, we have been witness to three trends which have had enormous impact on the function we categorize variously as public relations/public affairs/communications.

1. The concept of the world as a global market and the evolution of the multinational corporation to fulfill the needs of (and profit from serving) that market.

2. The recognition that the modern corporation is a social entity that not only must satisfy its stockholders, employees, and customers, but must also meet certain expectations placed on it by the societal structure in which it operates—and to do so not only in conformance with the letter, but also with the spirit of the law as well.

3. The advancing technology of communications which has integrated the world continent-to-continent, country-to-country to the point where news now transcends the boundaries of free-world nations virtually with the speed of light.

The modern corporation—nationality notwithstanding—is an organism with an inherent primary characteristic of adapting to the dynamic environment in which it operates. Survival is indeed a basic, genetic-like instinct.

It is therefore not surprising that corporations, through their public relations/public affairs/communications functions, have geared themselves to meet the new needs of social responsiveness and to survive the impact as well as exploit the capabilities of modern communications technology.

Nor is it surprising that different corporations—even those whose roots have a common nationality or serving the same industry or market—have met these new challenges differently. That their responses have differed reflects the competitive market system of much of the free world's business.

To catalog these differences, to explore the strategies a company applies to its public communications—and, most important, how it evolves its basic policy vis-a-vis its role in society—the Marsteller Foundation made its grant to the University of Illinois to enable the authors to meet first-hand in eight nations with leaders who handle public affairs for large multinational corporations.

Our interest in this subject is a natural evolution of the growth of Marsteller Inc. and Burson-Marsteller as advertising and public relations firms in overseas markets. Paralleling the experience of our clients—mainly multinational corporations—we have noted the growing concerns of business as a participant in an increasingly complex world society. How corporations have organized themselves to cope with newly-arising problems in the public affairs arena has been a subject to which we have paid close attention, both as advisor and as observer.

As one step in codifying experience from a cross section of corporate sources, we feel fortunate in having had the services of Dr. S. Watson Dunn, formerly of the University of Illinois and now Dean of the College of Business and Public Administration at the University of Missouri, to delve deeply into this subject with a variety of companies representing diverse national origins.

The results are in no way definitive. It was not expected that they would be. Rather, it is enlightening—and reconfirming of our faith in the competitive system—that individual corporations can achieve a somewhat equal measure of success in a variety of ways in recognizing their problems and developing programs to meet changing situations.

HAROLD BURSON
Chairman, Burson-Marsteller

Preface

In 1976 the directors of the Marsteller Foundation presented the author, then on the faculty at the University of Illinois at Urbana-Champaign, with two provocative questions that became the genesis of this study. The first was: Have any comprehensive studies been done on how sophisticated multinational corporations plan and carry out their global public affairs functions? The second question was: If the answer is negative, would such a study be productive and valuable to today's international executives?

To attempt to answer the first question, a study was undertaken to search current literature dealing with public affairs activities of multinational, or as some prefer to call them "transnational," corporations operating both in the United States and abroad.

We analyzed many articles and books dealing with the public affairs activities of leading multinationals. Some of these works are based on serious and methodical research, some are based mainly on theory, and some lean heavily on political bias—tending usually toward an antimultinational position. There were many contradictory opinions and findings. On the one hand, Richard J. Barnet and Ronald E. Muller, authors of *Global Reach: The Power of the Multinational Corporation* (New York: Simon and Schuster, 1974), accuse multinationals of putting headquarters profit before social responsibility to the host country. They cite certain "evidence" gained mainly from a survey of how multinationals operate in the developing countries. On the other hand, a study by David Blake indicates quite a different finding. The study concludes that multinationals do not really "manage" their international public affairs activities, that instead they let their subsidiaries manage that function without much in the way of goals or priorities from headquarters. Although studies have been done on how multinationals are organized for practice of their public relations activities, there was little on why they were organized as they were.

Based on our analysis of these and many other studies, we were forced to conclude that a serious lack of information prevails on how executives make decisions in their public affairs activities and why certain multinationals had weathered public affairs crises much more successfully than some of their competitors. With an enabling grant from the Marsteller Foundation, the project took shape and came to life.

This study was designed to answer such questions as: How do top managements identify and evaluate the public affairs problems their companies face abroad? What information do they seek and how do they use what they get? Why are some multinational corporations more successful than others in getting along with host governments abroad? Is socially responsible behavior compatible with profitable behavior? How do the more successful multinationals convey to the right audiences the story of their good deeds and reduce the impact of their mistakes? As we analyzed previous studies of multinationals and had preliminary conversations with corporation executives, it became clear that a study in depth would probably be more helpful than a broad survey. As a consequence, we decided to study a relatively few multinational corporations in detail and compile case histories on them.

The multinational corporations solicited for potential case histories were, for the most part, very large, quite experienced in international business, and generally regarded as sophisticated in their practice of public affairs. They had a good understanding of both the pitfalls and the many opportunities in international affairs. In a few cases the term "public affairs" caused confusion. Some executives preferred such terms as "external affairs" or the more general and traditional term, "public relations." Most, however, were quite conscious of the growing importance of the public affairs function and most had an executive designated to head this function. For the purpose of this study, the definition of "public affairs" developed by Caterpillar Tractor turned out to be a good one:

> . . . the planned effort to gain understanding and influence opinion inside and outside the company through (1) actions that are responsive to the public interest and (2) effective, two-way communications.

In selecting companies for our in-depth case studies, a special effort was made to include both industrial and consumer companies, although the operations of many large multinationals encompass both. A special effort also was made to include a variety of managerial styles. Moreover, we wanted companies based in a variety of industrialized countries of Western Europe as well as those based in the United States. In our sample of multinational firms, we believe a good balance was achieved of these various criteria. Of the fifteen companies included in this report, eight are based in the United States; seven are based in Western Europe.

In all cases, a researcher personally interviewed top executives as well as the executive in charge of the public affairs function. Each company's background was reviewed intensively, using both material released by the company itself and that available in independent outside media. Factual information in each case history was checked for accuracy by the company, but the opinions and interpretations presented in this report are entirely those of the authors.

All of us concerned with the study were pleased with the cooperation we received in our contacts with participating companies. Executives gave us masses of company materials, much of it confidential, so we could understand how the decision process really worked. They willingly searched for additional information when we returned to them for clarification of some of our preliminary impressions. We are deeply indebted to them, for, without their assistance, this study could not have been completed.

Corporations that declined to cooperate provided us with our first finding—that some prefer to keep a low profile and avoid drawing attention to the fact that their operations are so far-flung. This was especially true of certain European multinationals which have been expanding rapidly in recent years. As the executive of one pointed out, "You know and we know that we are a big multinational with holdings all over the world. But the people here at home don't really think of us as a multinational. And most people in the United States think of the companies we own there as U.S. companies."

Another finding that emerged from some early turndowns was that some of the most sophisticated multinationals think of what they do in public affairs as "proprietary" and are unwilling to share their "secrets." One multinational executive had granted preliminary approval for a case history but declined when he was overruled by a superior. The reason was that the company had encountered public affairs problems that were not widely known outside the company, and there was some fear that delving into these might prove embarrassing to the company.

Another conclusion derived from our early investigations is that handling of public affairs abroad is one of the most sensitive areas of today's multinational management. In one case, a European multinational company objected to our including a case that described a situation in which the company was receiving much unfavorable publicity in the European, but not the American, press. A strong effort was made by our research persons to include the company's as well as the critics' side of this story, but the multinational management still withheld approval. The firm's management had underestimated a situation that had started in Africa, had mushroomed to a cause célèbre in the European press, and was proving embarrassing to the firm.

We would like to give special recognition to the many people who helped make this study possible. Three of the cases were researched and prepared by Jean J. Boddewyn, Professor of International Business, Baruch School, City University of New York, who also served as an advisor on the remainder of the manuscript. Field and library research was undertaken by research assistants Julie Moser, Rose Ann Nagel, and Martin Gertler of the University of Illinois at Urbana-Champaign. The cases and introductory material were extensively edited by Martin Cahill on behalf of the Marsteller Foundation. Serving as coordinators on the project were Marsteller executives Robert Trebus and Joe Wilkerson. Always behind the scenes, providing encouragement and helpful comments, was Harold Burson, chairman of Burson-Marsteller, from whose inquisitive mind the project emanated.

S. WATSON DUNN

1

Overview

The phenomenal growth of multinational business enterprises over the past 24 years testifies to the compelling promise and opportunity in world markets. But this growth is not a simple expansion from domestic to world scale. The first thing a company finds when it ventures abroad is that things are different in other countries. It cannot operate abroad in exactly the same ways it operates at home.

These differences tend to occur primarily in three basic areas: business practices, cultural factors, and the objectives of the host government. Each country has its own special character and peculiarities in each of these areas that must be identified and dealt with if a company is to succeed.

Each of these three tends to fall into different areas of responsibility within a company. Business practices occur largely in the operational area; cultural factors relate largely to marketing; and government relations fit into the government affairs function.

But all three factors also interrelate. Sometimes a company has the best product in its field, manufactured under the best conditions, offered at the best price and with airtight guarantees and warranties and still fails to develop a viable market in a foreign country. This results sometimes from failure to relate properly to the cultural factors in the country, sometimes from failure to take into account the objectives and desires of the host government.

The critical nature of these interrelationships establishes the need for attention to public affairs in multinational corporations, and it clearly indicates the function's importance.

In fact, public affairs is so integral to success in the most successful multinationals that it is a major concern of top management. And

1

managers have a very clear idea of what they expect from their public affairs function: a sociopolitical environment in which the company can operate effectively. All public affairs activities are geared to this expectation. They are aimed at appropriately resolving conflicts or potential conflicts between the company's operations and the sociopolitical environment in each country in which the company operates.

If a conflict can be resolved before the situation becomes a major problem, so much the better. But, of course, this is not always possible. Sociopolitical forecasting is an imprecise art at best and there is no foolproof early warning system. Sometimes a problem erupts with no warning or before it can be contained and it must be dealt with as a crisis.

In either case—problem prevention or crisis management—the key words are "appropriate resolution." Public affairs is a pragmatic give-and-take proposition. Managers cannot expect their public affairs function to sell the company's point of view, regardless of what the circumstances may be in a given country. Managers recognize that they must give on occasion. How much they are willing to give—or can give without defeating their own purposes—defines the limits of "appropriate" in resolving any problem.

Measuring results of public affairs programs

If a company's policy is 100 percent ownership of all overseas operations, it is not going to be able to operate in some countries, no matter how much use it makes of public affairs techniques. The government in certain countries simply will not accept such an arrangement.

The success of a public affairs program must be based on carefully defined objectives realistically set for each country. If, for example, a country generally accepts fifty-fifty ownership and public affairs efforts result in the company holding 60 percent, those would be highly successful efforts. However, if the best the company could come away with was 40 percent ownership, the public affairs effort might be considered somewhat less than successful, but not an outright failure.

When the government of France decided to nationalize its telecommunications industry, International Telephone & Telegraph (ITT) sold all its interest in the industry to a French-owned company. Siemens, on the other hand, retained 30 percent ownership of its French holdings in the industry. ITT was satisfied because it protected its other operations in France. Siemens was satisfied because it retained a very lucrative piece of business. The government of France was satisfied because it had significantly furthered an important national goal.

Success of the public affairs effort can best be measured in terms of the give-and-take of the relative values involved. Management is in the best position to determine what is or what is not an appropriate resolution of the firm's difficulties. It is difficult, if not impossible, for an outsider to make such an assessment. It is not the intent of this book, therefore, to show public affairs "successes" that can necessarily be emulated and public affairs "failures" that should be avoided. As in marketing, research, production, and even in management, there are no simple, standard operating formulas for success in public affairs. We found that those managements that took this complexity into consideration and, as a consequence, conducted audits on a continuing basis were the most successful. Public affairs is perhaps the fastest-moving of the various areas in which management must make decisions.

What causes a need for public affairs activities?

While the public affairs functions in all multinationals are based on the same general goals or objectives, specific objectives and the approaches used to implement them vary widely. This is a result of the dynamics of the situations they encounter as they operate around the world.

Each company has distinctive characteristics, and these do not always mesh smoothly with the sociopolitical environment in a particular country. Five broad characteristics most often give rise to conflicts in implementing public affairs objectives: management objectives, products or services marketed, marketing interfaces, manufacturing and operations, and a characterisitic we can perhaps label "presence."

Of these, management objectives is the most significant in terms of public affairs needs. It is the single most important influence in most companies and situations.

In appraising the influence of these characteristics, one must keep in mind the danger of overreacting to criticism of multinationals by authors writing in the popular media and books and speeches by leftist politicians. It was evident that the executives in those firms most successful in their public affairs were quite realistic in their appraisal of how their various publics viewed their company. Often, careful research indicated that anti-multinational corporation feeling was not nearly so pervasive or so deep as articles and speeches might indicate.

Several (e.g., Henkel) decided that this hostility was based at least partly on ignorance. Those firms consequently made direct, friendly overtures to media critics with some success.

Management objectives

Those multinationals that were most successful usually had well-formulated public affairs objectives. These are most often based on the firm's management objectives. The chief executive can view the firm's problems from the top and can evaluate from that position the alternative ways in which trouble can be avoided. Every chief executive knows that if you go into the kitchen you are going to feel heat. The closer you get to the stove—where the main action is—the more intense the heat. Some managements prefer to skirt the edges of the kitchen and avoid some of the intense heat. Others set a bold, ambitious course, and, if it takes the company near the stove, so be it. Between these two poles are endless variations. Each creates quite different public affairs needs. Preventive public affairs action to avoid burns is generally recognized as the most desirable. But the bolder the management course, the more difficult this is and the greater the frequency of "firefighting" efforts to minimize burns.

The public affairs function must first be geared to respond to the specific needs created by such style. Management of the public affairs activity must chart and advise on courses of action that will minimize conflict and must be prepared to act effectively, anywhere in the world, when problems inevitably arise.

Products or services

Each product or service a company markets has an impact on the country in which it is sold. This impact can create critical public affairs needs. As has already been noted, the government of France decided that the impact of telecommunications was so sensitive that ownership should be French-controlled. In a less-developed country, the opposite might hold true. The country may desperately need a modern telecommunications system and welcome foreign producers that can supply their needs.

Similarly, jet fighters have a different impact from sewing machines in any given country. Basic products like automobiles or tractors have a different impact in a country that has no domestic production than in a country that is encouraging a budding industry.

The public affairs needs created by products or services can sometimes be identified and assessed in advance.

Citibank, for instance, makes an advance study of the economic objectives of a country, then constructs a financial services package it can offer that will help that country and its citizens achieve those objectives. Caterpillar takes a less specific approach. It studies world needs and develops products that will be useful in doing the work that will be required to meet those needs.

There is less flexibility in the design of a package for a piece of heavy equipment than in the design of a package of banking services. Caterpillar's approach may represent sound global marketing, but it may not always preempt public affairs problems in host countries as effectively as Citibank's tailored approach. This means that the public affairs people at Caterpillar will face different needs than will the people at Citibank.

Marketing Interfaces

Public affairs practitioners in companies that sell products to the public on the open market, either directly or through national dealers or distributors, cite this as an advantage in their work. For instance, Singer's public affairs manager feels the company is less vulnerable to the charges of corruption, bribery, and manipulation that so often beset companies that sell directly to or through the government.

This is, however, a matter of degree, and the degree of difference is shrinking. Government regulation of a product is not unlike government purchase of a product in terms of whether there will be a market for the product in the country. And government regulation of products—licensing and approving them for sale—is growing around the world.

When companies comment on the issue of relations with foreign governments, they insist they do not make "deals." Most have written corporate policies to this effect. Some, mostly American, have recently undertaken extensive internal studies to make certain the policy is actually being observed in all their operations around the globe.

The situation is not black and white, however. It is clouded by the question of what is "proper." Practices illegal in one country may be accepted ways of doing business in another. A company that adheres strictly to a policy of restraint may find itself at a serious disadvantage in some countries. A company that goes along with the accepted practices in a country may find it has a different problem. A number of American companies have been criticized at home for engaging in practices that are quite legal and above board in those countries where they were used but are illegal in the United States.

Another form of market interface occurs when public affairs activities must be coordinated with advertising and sales promotion. In the more successful multinationals, these functions are planned in conjunction with each other and the managers in charge of each are kept informed of what the others were doing. In the case of ITT, for example, the functions are all the responsibility of the senior vice president for advertising and public affairs. In some multinationals, however, the public affairs specialists and the marketing executives are on different wavelengths. In some cases, coordination is made difficult by the fact that the public affairs function is handled internally while advertising is handled externally through an advertising agency. Multinationals generally prefer a low profile for their corporation but a high profile for their brands.

Manufacturing and operations

A company's operations have varying impacts on the country in which they are located. The public affairs implications are manifold. Mining and oil production provide jobs but they also deplete natural resources. A chemical plant affects the environment. A bank may provide needed financial resources but it also may create financial dependence on a foreign-controlled institution. Where is the knowhow to rest in a high technology institution—exclusively with the foreign owners or shared with nationals in the host country?

How are the workers in a plant built by a foreign-based company to be dealt with and protected? And what about the management of the operation? Will top-level jobs be available to natives of the country or held only by foreigners?

Business cycles turn down at times. What happens when a plant no longer needs all the employees it has hired? Or if the plant has to close?

Every government and organized groups within each country have differing views on these questions. In some countries, a company cannot fire an employee without first obtaining government permission. In others, representatives of labor are required by law to have a voice at the board level.

The possibilities for conflict between company policy and customary practices in any country are almost unlimited. And this area is changing more rapidly, it seems, than any other. The importance of the social impact of operations introduced by multinationals in a country is well recognized. And it is giving rise to government actions to gain more control over the operations in the public interest.

Nationalism, the most extreme step in this direction, is of growing concern to multinational corporations.

Company presence

The preceding characteristics—management style, products or services, market interfaces, and manufacturing and operations—arise from the nature of the company's business. "Presence" deals more with the perception of the company by influential parties and groups in the host country. It is almost axiomatic that the larger and more visible the company's operations, the larger and more pressing are its needs in public affairs.

A company that has an insignificant share of the market and little visibility has little presence and usually is virtually unaffected by sociopolitical pressures in the host country. As it grows and prospers, however, it becomes more visible. Its impact on the country becomes more significant and more clearly defined. It develops a presence. And questions are raised in the public sector regarding it operations.

An example shows how presence affects public affairs needs. A country without development funds of its own encourages a hotel chain to come in to develop a tourist resort. Agreements are reached under very cordial circumstances. The concept is readily accepted by local citizens. And, as construction begins and jobs are created, everyone appears to be pleased with the arrangements. There are no public affairs problems.

But when the hotel is completed and tourists begin flocking in, the situation changes. The local citizens perceive little direct benefit themselves; the construction workers have been laid off. A few permanent jobs have been created in the hotel, perhaps, but that is mostly unskilled work. Not much in comparison to what the busy, apparently prosperous foreign hotel is doing. The hotel is bringing tourists in, as it said it would, but it appears that the money is going to the foreigners who own the hotel. And they're taking it right back out of the country.

This is a substantial increase in "presence," and it generates political pressure on the government. No matter what the economic facts are, the hotel owners begin to hear demands to renegotiate the original agreement on terms the host country considers more suitable for its citizens.

Presence is not always a matter of market share. The branch of a foreign-owned bank may require a large, highly visible building for its operations, even though it actually has only a 1 or 2 percent share of the market. Or a company's operations in a country may be almost insignificant, but its worldwide size and reputation may carry over and give it a presence far in excess of any market share it has in that country.

Presence develops in three stages. In the first, a company is introducing itself. Its efforts are largely marketing oriented, and public affairs efforts, if they exist, are directed to opening doors that will expand marketing horizons. The John Deere case in Part Six is a good example.

In the second stage, conflicts have arisen from the successful pursuit of opportunities created in the first stage. The company's presence has reached a critical mass and its impact is having repercussions. Public affairs efforts now take on a critical role. Valuable investments and markets are at stake. Public affairs focuses on consolidation and maintaining these valuable assets. BASF, also in Part Six, provides a typical example.

The third stage is one of maturity. This is evident in a number of companies that have been in international business for some time. The major adjustments have been made in the countries where they operate. They have worked things out, as it were. They have established relationships of mutual respect in the host countries. They are like old acquaintances. Differences of opinion still arise, but the parties now know each other well and they can find a solution without the fireworks. Singer's sewing machine operations cited in Part Five show typical characteristics of this stage.

Managing company characteristics

The best-managed multinationals try to forecast public affairs crises, and the ultimate achievement in public affairs is preventing problems. This is accomplished by managing the characteristics of the company in such a way that conflicts are avoided or resolved before they become problems. Pirelli, best known for its automobile tires, seems to have been able to accomplish the ultimate. It is worth taking a special look at Pirelli's experience.

Pirelli is composed of fifteen companies operating in nine countries. These companies are held by Société Internationale Pirelli, headquartered in Basel, Switzerland. The operating companies are organized as highly autonomous, local companies. While most are headed by Italians, all the work force and most of the management are nationals.

For the most part, the companies do not import or export. They manufacture products for sale in the host country.

The manufacturing operations—tires and electrical wire and cable—depend on two basic raw materials, rubber and copper. Pirelli owns no copper mines or rubber plantations. Nor is there consolidated buying by the parent company. Each affiliate buys what it needs on the world market.

The size of the staff of the parent company indicates how autonomous the operating companies are. The total staff includes only 30 people, 10 of whom are secretaries.

Ownership of the affiliates also is shared in the host country. Securities issued by the affiliates are held by private investors in most countries. In a few countries, the government is a participant. In total, Pirelli comes about as close as possible to being a national company in each country in which it operates.

With this approach, Pirelli has managed to avoid most major problems that face multinationals. And consequently, the company has no public affairs function as such.

It is unlikely that this happened by accident. A check through the company characteristics that give rise to public affairs requirements shows that each is pretty well taken care of in the way the company has conducted itself.

Management style seems to be moderate rather than bold. A keen sensitivity to public affairs concerns is reflected. The company's products—automobile tires and coated copper wire—are not controversial. Pirelli purposely does not engage in mining or growing rubber, operations that might create public affairs problems. Pirelli's marketing interfaces are primarily with the public, not government. Manufacturing plants and marketing operations are staffed almost entirely by nationals; ownership is shared with the citizens or government of the host country; there is little import or export business; and technology is freely available for purchase by any of the national companies. Moreover, Pirelli's presence is well tuned to the situation. In the United States, for instance, the company poses no threat to the domestic industry. In Italy, it is a leader.

One must conclude that at Pirelli all the necessary public affairs adjustments have been made between the company's operations and the sociopolitical environments in the countries where it operates. The company says it has no public affairs function. From the viewpoint of this study, it must be said that the company has one, indeed. It is conceived and conducted by the company management, and management has done a remarkable job.

With most multinationals, however, public affairs matters are not so simple. A company with a diverse line of products, operating in 100 or more countries, faces a mind-boggling array of public affairs needs. Mobil produces crude oil and ships, refines, and markets petroleum products and chemicals all over the world. The impact of these widely varied operations creates public affairs challenges of enormous proportions. A company that sets out to do business in other countries must expect these problems to arise as part of its total effort, and the company must gear up to deal with them if it is to succeed.

How multinational companies organize public affairs

Organization of the public affairs function follows need as perceived by management in the best-organized multinationals. Thus we see that while most multinational corporations are structured on a decentralized, profit-center basis, the public affairs function sometimes is not. At ITT, for example, operating managers are responsible for the profit performance of their units and have broad control over their operations, except for public affairs. All actions in this area must be cleared in advance with corporate headquarters. On occasion, public affairs actions are initiated and conducted by headquarters staff.

At Citibank, by contrast, profit-center managers maintain control over staffing, budgeting, and program planning for the public affairs function at their location.

Both approaches have inherent advantages and disadvantages. In the centralized public affairs operation, internal communications flow from the units to headquarters. Clearance and approval procedures at headquarters require a relatively large staff. In some companies, the headquarters staff maintains a foreign desk for each major overseas country or region, much like that of a government's department of state. The major obstacle in this kind of operation is time. Supervisors must constantly be alert to preventing procedures from getting in the way of prompt action when it is needed. The major benefit is control. Communications by the company and actions the company takes can be coordinated on a worldwide basis. Consistency and uniformity can be maintained. And, most important, action by one unit that may unbalance the objectives of another can be avoided.

The workings of a decentralized public affairs function are the opposite. The major flow of internal communications is from corporate headquarters to operating units. These communications have two purposes: the first is to sensitize and educate operating-unit managers on the intricacies and importance of public affairs. The second is to inform them of company policy and guidelines so they can act in accordance with management objectives. With this sensitivity, education, and information, managers at the operating unit level, it is hoped, will make appropriate public affairs decisions.

In decentralized operations, the headquarters staff specifically assigned full time to overseas operations is generally small, and the staffs at operating units around the world are larger.

The major reason given for decentralized operation is efficiency. Decisions can be made at the scene of the problem. While prompt, clearly directed action results from this approach, there are two major pitfalls. First, actions taken without higher review may inadvertently contradict a company's position in another part of the world. Second, a situation may not receive the attention it deserves. An operating unit manager is customarily evaluated and rewarded on the basis of profit performance. If the choice is between good public affairs and improved profitability, the decision usually favors profitability. If a public affairs problem results from the decision, it can be taken care of later, perhaps with some "free" help from corporate staff.

The importance of public affairs in international operations is so pervasive that even in decentralized public affairs organizations corporate headquarters becomes more actively involved at the operating unit level than in any other function—except profit performance. The corporate public affairs staff is never remote when a public affairs problem arises.

Placement of the chief public affairs officer varies in the company structure. In some companies the top public affairs officer reports directly to and has a close working relationship with the chief executive officer. In others, the public affairs officer reports through another senior official. Sometimes through a committee he or she reports to the chief executive officer and the governing board of the company. The reporting structure reflects the sensitivity of the company to public affairs matters. The more sensitive the company, the closer the working relationship between the chief officer and the top public affairs officer. And the closer this working relationship, the more influential the public affairs officer is in the company.

In a few of our study cases, the public affairs executive calls on outside counsel for help. More frequently these big firms do not. For example, John Deere uses an international public relations firm on several occasions in Western Europe while Caterpillar does not.

Few of the U.S. multinationals studied make much use of the various government offices abroad in connection with their public affairs problems. They contend generally that their own employees are better informed on what is happening than most of the U.S. government representatives. This attitude seemed to indicate the presence of an adversary relationship with government officials as well as certain disenchantment with the caliber of U.S. representatives abroad. Executives in European multinationals, on the other hand, have a somewhat higher regard for officers of their governments stationed in foreign countries.

Three basic elements of public affairs in multinational corporations

Three basic elements are common to the public affairs functions of most multinational companies studied in this project. They are affirmative action, problem prevention, and crisis containment. Each component or action plan in each company's public affairs program relates to one or more of these elements. The total effort represented by each program is aimed at providing satisfactory coverage in all three elements. The first element works toward a general atmosphere. The other two deal with specific issues.

Affirmative action. This is an ongoing effort to create a generally favorable climate for the company's operations. Affirmative action is a communications and educational activity that encompasses external policy-making bodies within governments of host countries and within supranational organizations, such as the United Nations and the European Economic Community; key groups that influence policy within the countries, such as labor, public interest groups, and the press; and key audiences within the company—customers, employees, and stockholders.

Problem prevention. This function entails monitoring emerging situations to identify those that could adversely affect company operations. This is followed by an assessment of the potential impact of adverse situations, with an analysis of options and with recommendations on preventive action for defensive measures. Once a plan of action is agreed upon, the public affairs function ensures that it is carried out. .

Crisis containment. This is the quick, resourceful, effective response to critical situations that erupt without warning or before they can be contained. Usually the same procedures are followed as in problem prevention: analysis, recommendations, implementation. But these things are done under pressure. There is no time to become an expert in the country's affairs. That homework must have been done previously.

Placement of responsibility for these basic elements varies from headquarters in centralized public affairs functions to operating units in decentralized operations. But all functions have them. They constitute the ABCs of public affairs in multinational corporations. The experience of the companies reviewed in this study shows that, properly staffed and funded to cover those three basic elements, the public affairs function can make a significant contribution to the company's performance in the markets of the world.

The subsequent chapters cover case studies describing how fifteen major multinational companies organize and conduct their public affairs functions. The cases have been organized into six parts: the cases in the first part illustrate some of the effects of the all-important influence of management objectives. The cases in Part Two show some of the approaches to organizing and fixing responsibility within the company and the effect of these organizational variations on the function itself. The next four parts encompass cases which show how the other company characteristics described in this overview can affect the public affairs function.

Each case, however, does more than illustrate the central point of the part in which it appears. In all the cases, we attempt an overview of the public affairs function within the company. As a consequence, they reflect points made in other parts and show how all these influences are coordinated and accommodated in the total public affairs operation.

Part One

How management objectives affect public affairs

Management objectives are clearly the basic influence on every public affairs function in the multinational companies studied. In the two cases that follow, different approaches are taken, though management objectives are similar.

At Caterpillar Tractor Company and at Henkel, we find the same basic management objective: orderly, long-term growth, and expansion of international markets. Both companies recognize that this depends on more than good products, fair prices, and efficient management. While these are essential, the companies have identified another critical factor: strong company acceptance in the countries in which they operate.

Winning and holding this acceptance appears to be the major thrust of the public affairs function at both companies. But the companies take different approaches to this objective. Caterpillar builds its program around a code of conduct; the company's aim is to establish a single, worldwide standard for its operations. Henkel delegates policy making to the country or product group manager, and standards are set in relation to conditions in a given country rather than in accordance with a worldwide ideal. The case studies indicate that either approach works.

2

Caterpillar Tractor Company

"Improving the quality of life"

> World sales: $7.2 billion
> Percent sales abroad: 48
> Number of employees: 88,010
> Countries with subsidiaries: 15
> Central office: United States

Caterpillar Tractor Company is the second largest exporter of all U.S. corporations. Annual sales are well in excess of $7 billion; the company has 13 major manufacturing plants in the United States and 13 plants in 10 countries outside the United States. The company employs 88,000 persons worldwide. Its products—tractors, heavy equipment, and auxiliaries for agriculture, construction, and industry—are sold in virtually every country in the world through a network of some 230 independent dealers.

The role that public affairs is intended to play at Caterpillar has been clearly and carefully thought out. This is the company's definition of public affairs: the planned effort to gain understanding and influence opinion—inside and outside the company—through (1) actions that are responsive to the public interest, and (2) effective two-way communications.

The phrase "actions that are responsive to the public interest" is used in the broadest sense. It does not refer simply to public affairs activities. It refers to all actions of the company.

This position derives directly from management objectives and has been expanded into a comprehensive, clearly focused program practiced wherever the company conducts business. To achieve orderly, long-term growth, worldwide, the company believes it is as important to act in the public interest as it is to act in its own interest.

A great deal of thought has gone into the relationship between public and company interests at Caterpillar. This thinking encompasses basic philosophical and ethical principles. The company has concluded that as a matter of practical business it must set clear, high standards for itself in all areas of its operations and it must consistently adhere to these standards.

The thinking that led to this conclusion is summed up by one of the company's top public affairs executives: "Experience dictates that the lower the standards, the greater the risk—companies who are in trouble are largely those who failed to set their standards high enough and, instead, practiced situational ethics." Caterpillar is determined not to be among those companies that find themselves "in trouble."

Caterpillar pursues its convictions with single-minded dedication. In 1974 the company published a "Code of Worldwide Business Conduct." Copies of the code were distributed to each of its 13,000 managers around the world. The code sets forth in clear, simple terms the principles managers are expected to follow in all their business dealing.

In his introductory comments to managers, the chairman of the board talks about the spirit, not the letter of the code: "Of course, this code is not an attempt to prescribe actions for every business encounter. It is an attempt to capture the basic, general principles to be observed by Caterpillar people everywhere.

"To the extent our actions match these high principles, such can be a source of pride. To the extent they don't (and I'm by no means ready to claim perfection), these standards should be a challenge to each of us."

The code is a working document and managers are expected to meet its challenge. Under procedures formalized in 1977, at the end of each year each manager must file a report on compliance with the code. In this report, the manager affirms that he or she is familiar with the code and understands it. The manager then reports any occurrence that was or could be construed as a departure from the code. There can be no doubt among company managers that Caterpillar intends the code to be used and followed, not just read and then set aside.

The code covers virtually every facet of business operations, and the standards are indeed high. The code was revised in 1977, and there was no retreat from previously stated principles. Indeed, the few revisions and additions reflect further clarification and definition of the company's stand on issues that have received increasing attention since the code was first published.

Caterpillar is careful to note that the company is not trying to impose its code on others: "It is not our aim to attempt to remake the world in the image of any one country; rather, we would hope to help improve the quality of life, where we do business, by serving as a means of transmission and application of knowledge that has been found useful elsewhere."

A distinctive view

Despite the disclaimer, this view of the international enterprise has an idealistic flavor, almost a missionary zeal, especially when compared to what appears to be a more direct, realistic and practical approach followed by other multinationals. It even seems somewhat incongruous when one thinks of Caterpillar's best-known product—heavy earth-moving equipment—and the hardy people who buy and use these machines.

But Caterpillar disagrees with any suggestion that its approach is anything other than pragmatic. Its position, the company maintains, is based on sound, hard business considerations. Two examples help clarify this. A Caterpillar task force devoted two years to a study of world energy needs. Following the study, the company began aligning its capabilities to serve specific requirements it had identified for energy production equipment. This included the development and introduction of new products. This effort began well before the OPEC oil embargo.

History has proved that this was an effort in the public interest. But the effort also proved to be good, sound business practice—anticipate market needs and be ready to meet them as they arise.

The company completed another study in 1975 on world food supplies. This study also uncovered evolving needs—needs that Caterpillar has the capabilities, and now the intention, to meet.

Which comes first in these instances? Improving the quality of life or meeting market opportunities? Do the same principles guide planning for the future that are cited in evaluating past activities? And does it matter? Caterpillar is demonstrating that the basic business of business—serving markets—is not incompatible with serving human needs. In Caterpillar's view, the two go hand in hand. This has to be recognized as a sound and effective, perhaps even powerful, public affairs platform.

Organization of public affairs

Staffing and organization of the public affairs function follow the needs dictated by this assignment of responsibility. The central function is at company headquarters in Peoria, Illinois. The manager of public affairs has global responsibility for determining policy and for monitoring implementation. In the United States the manager also has direct responsibility for implementation.

The corporate public affairs department is organized into six divisions: public information, corporate and financial communications, employee information, governmental relations, community affairs, and contributions. (The company's code expressly prohibits political contributions; it is, however, a strong supporter of work in social, health, and educational areas.)

At the operating unit level, similar functions are established in the personnel departments. These staffs report to the plant manager who has local responsibility for supporting and implementing corporate policy.

Public affairs staff people in the operating unit are, for the most part, nationals of the country in which they work. This practice provides necessary insights into and sensitivity to the customs and practices of the host country. All local public affairs staff persons have spent considerable time at corporate headquarters in Peoria, Illinois. During this time, emphasis is on increasing their familiarity with how the company thinks and works. Improving communications skills is of secondary importance.

Corporate staff persons provide consulting services and policy guidance for operating units. They also monitor and audit performance of the operating units, working with local management to ensure adequacy of performance. A European public affairs manager serves as an extension of the corporate public affairs department, acting as consultant for public affairs staffs at European plants and providing liaison with the corporate public affairs department in Peoria.

The organization in action

An example illustrates how this organization works. When the issue arose of the United Kingdom joining the European Economic Community, Caterpillar had no position on the matter. The company had important operations in England and its employees there were divided on the issue. The problem was identified and evaluated by the operating unit public affairs staff in Great Britain. All opinions were solicited. A recommended position was developed and forwarded to corporate headquarters for review.

Caterpillar's corporate policy supports free trade. This dictated a position favoring the United Kingdom's entry into EEC, and that was the position taken by the company. Once the position was adopted, communications programs to explain it were initiated in Great Britain. These were directed to employees and the public. Other operating units affected by the issue and corporate headquarters also participated in the communications plan.

Room for disagreement

What happens when a manager disagrees with the company's position on an issue? The code of conduct is clear on this point: "Managers should feel a special obligation to the extent they identify themselves or may be identified with the company to give support to the company's beliefs.

"An employee who does not agree in principle with the company position on an issue should feel free to express his or her opposing views unless such expression interferes with his or her ability to fulfill job responsibilities. In such a case, the employee should speak as a private citizen and not as a representative of Caterpillar."

How company positions are established

One of the major functions of the corporate public affairs office is to establish company positions on specific major issues. These positions are set forth in internal bulletins prepared by the governmental affairs division. The company concentrates on issues that directly affect company operations or that would affect the business climate in which the company operates. In these positions, Caterpillar strives to reflect what in its view is best in the public interest as well as its own. It seeks to avoid hard-line advocacy of its own interests, regardless of public interest. When the company takes a position, it does not draw back if the issue is controversial.

In drafting positions, the public affairs office draws on the background and skills of both the corporate and the operating-unit staffs. Other pertinent areas of expertise within the company are also tapped. Departments ranging from environment, tax, and finance to sales and engineering may be involved in arriving at a recommended position on an issue.

Once a draft is prepared by the governmental relations department, the recommended position is reviewed. When approved, it becomes the company position. If the position is a new one, the chairman of the board must approve it.

An approved position serves as the basis for action. If such a position relates to legislative action in the United States, for instance, it may be advocated before legislators and committees, in the press, and before influential audiences in speeches by company executives. It may also be communicated to employees and shareholders through existing internal communications channels.

If appropriate and applicable, similar actions are undertaken by the staffs at operating units. Specific actions and target audiences will be adjusted as needs dictate.

In effect, the Caterpillar public affairs function operates on a centralized policy basis with decentralized implementation.

Pluses and minuses

The principles set forth in the Caterpillar code are far-ranging. They deal with 16 categories:

1. Ownership and investment in other countries
2. Location and operation of company plants and facilities
3. Relations with employees
4. Product quality
5. Sharing of technology
6. Finance
7. Intercompany pricing
8. Accounting and financial records
9. Observing differing business practices from one country to another
10. Competitive conduct
11. Observance of local laws
12. Business ethics
13. Relationships with public officials
14. Public responsibility
15. Disclosure of information
16. International business operations

In these principles, the company bases its position on the free enterprise system and an espousal of basically American ethical standards. Despite the code's recognition of other cultures and customs, some of which may not be compatible with the principles upheld by Caterpillar, an outside observer may wonder how viable and durable these principles are in the give-and-take of international commerce. Moreover, questions might be raised about the importance of doing so. What does it contribute? Is it worth it?

There are obvious risks in promulgating flatly stated principles. Caterpillar recognizes these major risks. By setting such high public standards for itself, the company sets itself up for sharp criticism, loss of credibility, even ridicule, should a flagrant abuse by a company official be revealed. The company's internal audit and reporting system is designed to discover such occurrences, if they exist.

What if the internal system uncovers a "scandal"? The CEO has a ready answer: "That would prove the system is working."

What if the audit and reporting system fails to spot a major violation and it is uncovered and revealed by an outsider? Caterpillar does not expect that to happen.

Dealers aligned to standards

Another line of questioning explores the possibility of an escape hatch for Caterpillar. Even if one accepts Caterpillar's high standards, there are the company's independent dealerships around the world. The skeptic might ask what control Caterpillar has over them so far as its code is concerned. And how is one outside the company, a customer, for instance, to know the difference? Do the dealers provide an escape hatch that enables the company to maintain its code and, at the same time, do what needs to be done in this or that country?

Caterpillar maintains that its dealers do not provide an escape hatch at all. The company's public affairs director puts it this way: "Like Caterpillar, they are in business for the long pull and there is much more to lose than to gain by unethical practices." In fact, Caterpillar urges its dealers to adopt written codes like its own, effectively cutting off any "out" they might provide.

Can dealers front for Caterpillar in under-the-table deals? The code covers this, too: "Caterpillar employees will take care to avoid involving the company in any such activities (bribes or kickbacks) engaged in by others. We won't advise or assist any purchaser of Caterpillar products, including dealers, in making or arranging such payments. We will actively discourage dealers from engaging in such practices."

Apart from these questions, other issues are based on practical business considerations. Business practices vary from one country to another. Customarily, managers are expected to adapt to these local practices and make the best of the situation. At Caterpillar, strict limits are imposed on adapting. For example: "We support laws of all countries which prohibit restraint of trade, unfair practices, or abuse of economic power. And we avoid such practices in areas of the world where laws do not prohibit them." Moreover, "Payments of any size to induce public officials to fail to perform their duties—or to perform them in an incorrect manner—are prohibited. Company employees are also required to make good faith efforts to avoid payment of gratuities or 'tips' to certain public officials, even where such practices are customary. Where these payments are as a practical matter unavoidable, they must be limited to customary amounts and may be made only to facilitate correct performance of the officials' duties."

Such restrictions don't make a local manager's job easier. And if competitors proceed according to permissive local law and custom, it is conceivable that the local Caterpillar manager be at a serious competitive disadvantage. Practically speaking, is this the better approach?

While Caterpillar concedes the possibility of short-term delays and inconveniences, it believes the longer-term results are well worth the effort. It has encountered situations where its code was simply not believed and accepted. In such situations, Caterpillar sticks by its principles until the other parties are convinced. After such a "get-acquainted" period, the company finds that a trust and understanding have been established that permit things to proceed at least as rapidly as they might have otherwise.

This is what Caterpillar's management is after: solid, long-term growth relationships. The practicality of the approach is demonstrated in the company's operating results.

For all the limitations placed on company actions by Caterpillar's code, it leaves considerable latitude for accommodating the varying needs and desires of governments and peoples around the world. Caterpillar prefers to own 100 percent of its overseas subsidiaries. Yet its code states: "Caterpillar investments must be compatible with the social and economic priorities of host countries and with local custom, tradition, and sovereignty."

This leaves room for the negotiation and accommodation necessary for doing business around the world. Caterpillar has wholly owned subsidiaries in eight countries outside the United States and joint ventures in Japan and India.

Potential pitfalls exist in Caterpillar's approach to public affairs. And there is room for skepticism. But the approach is as distinctive as the bright yellow color of Caterpillar's best-known products. And it seems to be working. In 1977, sales were more than double those in 1971. The major contributor to this growth was international business. Even the most skeptical would have difficulty finding fault with results like that.

3

Henkel KGaA

"A group of national companies"

World sales:	$3.15 billion
Percent sales abroad:	53
Number of employees:	34,000
Countries with subsidiaries:	90
Central office:	Federal Republic of Germany

Henkel KGaA competes with Procter & Gamble, Unilever, and Colgate-Palmolive in the world soap and detergent markets. The company is the largest producer and marketer in West Germany of detergents and cleansing and dishwashing agents. Founded over 100 years ago, Henkel today ranks among the largest family-owned companies in the world.

The company's headquarters and largest production facilities are in Dusseldorf. About 14,000 employees work in these installations, and 6,000 employees are at various other facilities in Germany. Another 14,000 employees work in manufacturing and sales operations in more than 40 countries outside Germany, and international operations account for more than 50 percent of total company sales.

Henkel's approach to public affairs is centralized information gathering, centralized planning, and local administration. Corporate policy is set by the management board. A 20-person Direktorium implements it. In subsidiaries in other countries, policy is set by the general manager and implemented by staff. The corporate staff supervises and assists subsidiary staff activities. The public affairs function is strictly one of implementation.

The public affairs staff is also largely responsible for gathering and analyzing information. In Germany, for instance, a detailed analysis of antibusiness attitudes was begun in 1970. Henkel is particularly concerned with this issue because the company is one of the country's largest advertisers and a frequent target for antibusiness sentiment.

Analyzing the situation

The fact finding began with a comprehensive attitude study of the company's image. Research showed that "pacesetter" groups, which largely determine sociopolitical opinion in Germany, had quite different views of the company than did the public at large. Many of the so-called pacesetters are leftist journalists, politicians, university professors, students, teachers, trade unionists, and public authorities. Persons from these groups gave the company low marks for progressiveness and up-to-date thinking. Many also questioned whether the company was completely attuned to their views on the role of corporations in society. These weak points in Henkel's image seemed to come primarily from a lack of information on the company, its management, its business operations, and company philosophy.

Several conclusions were drawn from this. First, additional communication with these groups was required. Second, favorable public opinion no longer depended solely on the quality of a company's products and the success of its business operations; especially important was the company's attitude toward society and its problems. Third, Henkel's position on problems facing society must be the major content of communications to the pacesetter groups.

Planning based on facts

From these observations, Henkel public relations people moved to specific concepts based on further investigation, input from certain influential groups, and staff evaluations:

Concept 1. Public opinion, in particular that of critical influential groups, is increasingly that sociopolitical responsibility of a company will be a moral prerequisite for doing business.

Concept 2. The reputation of the Henkel company, its progressiveness, its openness toward society and its problems, and its feeling of social responsibility toward its own employees and consumers are not recognized or are only partially recognized by particular influential groups. At times these are openly disputed.

Concept 3. In the past, Henkel's own social and sociopolitical convictions were not publicized at all.

When these findings and concepts were brought before the management board, they were accepted, and public relations was instructed to develop a campaign to deal with the situation.

The campaign was designed to define in the public eye and in the view of Henkel employees, Henkel's attitude toward fundamental problems of the economy and society. The backbone of the campaign was a series of advertisements. A press release announcing the series said: "In its advertising campaign, Henkel lays down the guidelines for its commercial activities within a changing society and the new turns the economy is taking. The statements in the advertisements . . . are to be taken as Henkel's opinion of itself."

The ad copy was straightforward and candid. It did not attempt to duck the tough questions. These are typical headlines:

Companies that think only in terms of profit will soon have a great deal to lose.

Companies that do not remain open to suggestions will soon have a lot less to say in matters.

Companies are a part of society, so they must also adopt an attitude to the problems of society.

Companies that do not take the consumer into account today will have to pay for it tomorrow.

Companies that take the easy route with their products will find the road increasingly hard.

Pretesting Impact

After these headlines were chosen and copy developed, it became clear that Henkel was breaking new ground for companies in West Germany. For this reason, Henkel submitted the advertisements to a preliminary test of 40 people. The group was composed solely of critical, influential people. The test was conducted by a Frankfurt opinion research firm. The test result was positive for both the content and the presentation of the material. The decision was made to proceed with the full-scale campaign.

The advertisements were published in media most influential with the target audience: national newspapers, newsmagazines, economic journals, and consumer and student newspapers. All advertisements were also printed in Henkel's employee newspapers.

Response was highly positive. Detailed and thoughtful comments by distinguished press bodies indicated they had scrutinized the ads carefully. Comments also indicated the press believed it interesting and noteworthy that a company should concern itself so openly with the problems of society and the economic structure. They used such adjectives as "adventurous," "progressive," and "exemplary."

The ads met with similar response in economic and political circles, and the public relations director received a number of important invitations to appear at conferences to explain the background and development of the campaign.

Adaptable technique

A similarly direct though less-elaborate approach was followed in dealing with a similar attitude in France. An antibusiness attitude was becoming increasingly pronounced in the French press, and Henkel was attracting some of the fire. Perhaps the most influential French newspaper, *Le Monde,* carried an article about Henkel, raising the question: "Why should a company of 34,000 employees be owned by one family?"

The general manager in France suggested that top company management invite a key editor from *Le Monde* to Dusseldorf for interviews and personal inspection of the company. The management board approved the idea, and the then head of operations and marketing issued a personal invitation.

The editor was interested but insisted on guarantees of interviews with top management. These arrangements, along with preliminary backgrounding sessions with the editor in Paris, were handled by Henkel's public relations manager in France.

The result was a long article in *Le Monde*, depicting Henkel fairly and accurately. Henkel executives felt it was, on balance, not anti-Henkel and probably helped to improve the company's image in France.

The handling of this situation reflects the company's operating practices in the area of public affairs. The initiative came from the general manager in the country involved. Corporate headquarters approved and provided the requested cooperation. The public affairs official in the country that had the problem handled the details.

Environment gets special attention

Henkel has a highly organized approach for what it considers the most pressing worldwide public affairs problems it faces, namely, environmental protection. Because of the nature of the company's products and the conditions of manufacturing them, this problem exists in virtually every country where the company operates.

Henkel believes the United States has the most advanced programs for environmental controls. It recently acquired General Mills Chemicals, Inc., which was merged with the former Henkel, Inc., company into the new Henkel Corporation (based in Minneapolis, Minnesota). It also has acquired a 20 percent interest in Clorox. These provide it with a valuable window on U.S. developments. Henkel views these as indications of what to expect in other areas. Along with this inside view, the company also gains a great deal of information on how to deal with problems—information it believes it can use in other parts of the world.

In Europe, environmental protection programs vary widely from country to country, but the problems are similar to those in the United States. Efforts are already under way within the European Economic Community that will lead to more uniform and stricter programs throughout Europe.

To monitor the evolving situation, Henkel has organized a committee on environmental problems. This committee of six top executives includes the head of the public relations department. The committee gathers information from all countries in which Henkel operates, evaluates it, and develops recommendations in three areas: what public relations steps should be initiated; what chemical research should be undertaken to resolve questions; and what potential economic impact various issues might have on Henkel.

The company has developed and is applying technology for removing air and water pollutants from its manufacturing operations, but it has not yet worked out an international plan for environmental action. Because the needs and requirements vary so widely from one country to another, Henkel believes that at this point a more effective and responsive approach is to deal with each situation on the same basis, country by country, under the direction of the country manager with assistance in the form of counsel or work force as required from Dusseldorf.

Motivate rather than control

The public affairs function at Henkel is typical of many European multinationals. Public affairs is regarded as a line responsibility. It is the responsibility of top operating management and country managers. They set policy and priorities. The staff administers their directives.

Even with problems shared by many locations, such as environmental protection, the manager in a given country maintains responsibility and control. The corporation acts as a monitor and review board for planning and as a resource for implementation.

Henkel has found that this approach meets its needs very well and there are no plans to change it. The corporate director of public affairs believes the company's policy conforms ideally to worldwide pressures on companies to place authority and responsibility in their national subsidiaries.

"In view of this," he says, "the public relations department will continue to regard itself and act as coordinator and catalyst rather than a control center. And last but not least, as a turnstile for the necessary exchange of information."

Part Two

Organization of the public affairs function

Companies vary widely in how they position public affairs responsibility and authority. On the one extreme is tight, centralized control;
on the other is a decentralized, operation-oriented organization.

Centralized control can be maintained in several ways. At ITT,
authority is vested in a strong manager who controls activities from
company headquarters. Siemens takes another approach. The company has no formal public affairs function. Policy authority is vested
in management, and centralized control is maintained through the
management structure. Various staff functions—communications,
advertising, personnel, finance, and legal—carry out management's
programs.

Citibank, on the other hand, decentralizes the public affairs operation. The senior banking officer at the local level controls objectives,
program planning, budgeting, and staffing. Corporate staff sets standards and provides counsel and specialized communications services.

The following studies illustrate how the organizational structure
affects the flow of internal communications and staff requirements.

31

4

International Telephone & Telegraph Corporation

For timely corporate disclosure everywhere,
New York headquarters calls the shots.

World sales: $19 billion
Percent sales abroad: 50
Number of employees: 375,000
Countries with subsidiaries: 80
Central office: United States

International Telephone & Telegraph Corporation (ITT) has 250 subsidiaries and divisions employing over 375,000 people in 80 countries around the world. Most corporate communications issued from all these locations are first reviewed, approved, and timed for release at ITT headquarters in New York.

Communications deemed particularly sensitive are not only approved in New York, their release and distribution are handled there, too, rather than from the location where the news originates, as is customary.

An example of such a sensitive situation occurred when the company entered into negotiations to sell its controlling interest in the French-based Le Matériel Téléphonique to Thomson CSF, a French electronics company. The negotiations were undertaken at the strong urging of the French government. Le Matériel Téléphonique was a major manufacturer in telecommunications, an industry the government had determined should be entirely French owned.

The situation was complicated and highly sensitive. The French government did not want to get a reputation for forcing foreign investors to sell profitable operations to French companies. ITT did not want to antagonize the French government and jeopardize its other sizable operations there.

In addition, ITT had a potential problem with its shareholders. The Ministry of Post and Telecommunications in France had recently announced that an ITT switching system was one of two adopted for installation throughout the country. This represented a sizable piece of profitable business. Would the shareholders suffer if ITT sold off the company that would control this business?

33

Thomson, of course, also had its business interest to protect. Some 8,500 French citizens were employed by Le Matériel Téléphonique. This highly skilled labor pool was a significant factor in Thomson's interest in the acquisition. A period of uncertainty could mean the departure of the most valued of these employees.

The principals determined that, in this situation, the premature release of information before final agreements were reached could only lead to trouble; no one would benefit from rumor, speculation, charges, and countercharges. The principals agreed, therefore, that information would be released only when it was complete and accurate. ITT assumed responsibility for handling the release of any and all information.

Dateline: New York

To ensure absolute control, ITT decided that just one person would act as spokesperson and source of information on the subject. That was a senior staff member of the Corporate Relations and Advertising Deparment in New York.

The ITT negotiator for the sale, an executive vice-president from New York headquarters, called the corporate offices every day from France to report on progress. The head of ITT in France also made daily calls to New York headquarters, reporting on rumors and press reports relating to the negotiations.

ITT legal and financial staffpersons reviewed all information and forwarded it with their comments to the spokesperson. Only after the boards of directors of both ITT and Thomson CSF had approved the final agreement was it felt that complete and accurate information could be disclosed.

At that time, a one-page news story was released simultaneously around the world. Requests for additional information were referred to the designated spokesperson in New York.

ITT listed on ten exchanges

ITT securities are listed on ten major exchanges around the world and each exchange has its requirements for disseminating material information. ITT, therefore, must be particularly sensitive about any information that could be subject to these regulations or affect the markets for its stock. The simple difference in time between New York and London, say, or Tokyo, makes meeting disclosure requirements extremely complicated.

Timing, perhaps more than any other factor, dictates the

company's strict policy on centralized control of information to the press. Such control does not necessarily extend to the promotion of products or services, of course. It is restricted to *corporate* information. But policy and guidelines are clearly set forth, and all ITT managers around the world are obliged to observe the policy.

The policy statement on this matter is clear and explicit. There is little if any room for uncertainty or confusion. It covers news releases, speeches, articles for publication, and even inadvertent or accidental disclosure.

Policy guidelines but no code

While ITT does not have a written over-all public affairs code, certain deductions can be made from the policy statements that do exist: the basic conclusion drawn from a review of materials is that primary emphasis is placed on the financial aspects of business. All other considerations take on importance insofar as they relate to fiscal matters.

A strong case can be made for this point of view. For example, it could be constructed like this:

The role of a business enterprise in society is to generate economic wealth. It does this by purchasing raw materials, equipment, and supplies; by creating jobs and paying wages; by producing and selling products; and by realizing a profit to return to investors.

It is the role of other institutions in society—government, for instance—to monitor and regulate these activities to ensure that the business enterprise does not generate economic benefits at the expense of other benefits to which society is entitled.

These are, in short, naturally adversary roles.

In the give-and-take of day-to-day operations as these adversaries pursue their goals, they move toward a middle ground—the interaction of business and society that is called public affairs.

If this is the basic philosophy of ITT management—and there is much to indicate that it is—it is not surprising to find that the company's basic policy on disclosure of information is dictated by financial and legal considerations. If the basic operating policy of the company is built on what will best advance the economic goals of the total company (in the most expeditious and orderly manner consistent with legal and regulatory requirements), the communications practices of the company will follow suit.

Making a code?

ITT helped formulate the viewpoint advocated by the United States in the preparation of the Office for Economic Cooperation and Development (OECD) Guidelines for Multinational Enterprises. Nevertheless, the company remains very much concerned about the disclosure requirements that may emerge in the final document. As currently stated, these requirements, ITT feels, probe far beyond what is really needed for proper governmental supervision and do little to correct what the company views as an imbalance in present disclosure practices that puts U.S. multinationals at a competitive disadvantage.

ITT states its position this way: "Our concern is that American multinational corporations now disseminate more information than their European counterparts. While the promulgation of the OECD guidelines might help balance that, there are many who believe that European multinational corporations may not comply because the guidelines have no sanction or authority."

In the meantime, ITT continues to release information that contributes to this imbalance (sometimes including information it would prefer to keep within the company) because it is required to do so by one or another of the jurisdictions under which it operates. These concessions illustrate how the adversary give-and-take works. ITT will do what must be done to operate in those countries and markets in which it believes it can profitably do business.

While some companies (Caterpillar, for instance) believe they should consistently apply a home-grown business code to operations around the world, others hold that it is more appropriate to follow whatever practices are common in the host country. With the recent passage of U.S. legislation regarding questionable payments, all American companies are now operating under one uniform code.

Finding a happy medium

In practice, neither approach can be followed in its purest sense. A code is an ideal and the people who are to practice the code are human. Caterpillar acknowledges this and affirms that its code leaves room for "sinners." And those operating around the opposite pole can discover that they are not entirely free of business regulations just because they have stepped offshore. Revelations of payments by American multinationals to high officials of foreign governments have caused a number of companies to adopt at least part of a code.

This is what happened at ITT. Early in 1975, after ITT was

accused (along with several other U.S. multinationals) of making questionable payments in several foreign countries, the ITT board of directors authorized the general counsel of the corporation and Davis, Polk, and Wardwell, independent counsel to the board, to review the practices of ITT and its 250 subsidiaries and divisions around the world. The review spanned five full years, from 1971 through 1975.

ITT disclosed the findings in the company's 1975 annual report. On the subject of political contributions, a change in corporate policy resulted. The annual report stated that during the period of the study $4,300 had been contributed for U.S. political events and $60,000 contributed to political parties in countries where such practices were legal.

In 1975, the company issued a policy memorandum making it clear that no contribution to political parties or candidates will henceforth be made, even where it is legal to do so.

What's a bribe?

The report gave more attention to the question of "bribes." During the five-year period, gross sales had approached $50 billion. In examining the sales practices involved, the report stated that the company had paid a total of $3.8 million in addition to customary sales commissions to "assist in developing or improving business relationships" in host countries. The report also stated that "with minor exceptions" the company was not aware of any illegal or improper practices engaged in by sales agents. Expediting business often is a judgment factor for local managements to reckon with. No change in corporate policy was deemed necessary.

The report points out: "In many areas of the world, it is not unusual, and often accepted as normal practice, to give presents or make payments of modest value to government functionaries to expedite administrative action or secure procedural assistance." Such payments were not significant, according to ITT.

When in Rome . . .

In conclusion, the general policy of the company was reaffirmed by the board of directors: "All future activities of each unit of the ITT system throughout the world (will) comply with the law and ethical practices in the jurisdiction in which the unit operates."

Beginning with the premise that the purpose of an enterprise is to make profit within the limits of the law, it is difficult to fault this position. Indeed, it appears that the position could only be faulted by those who see broader responsibilities inherent in the conduct of a business. While this book does not attempt to evaluate that issue, it is obvious that each company management must resolve its own position on this basic point before it can develop consistent policy on public affairs and communications practices.

Communications management

As noted, the communications policy of ITT calls for tight, centralized control. ITT management has concluded that it is not practical to expect the manager in Berlin to know what is going on in Hong Kong, Sydney, or Mexico City. Nor can the manager be expected to interpret how these activities interrelate with his or her own operation in the interest of advancing the corporate goals. Therefore, the manager cannot be expected to gauge accurately the worldwide impact of public statements about his or her operations. As a consequence, what the manager intends to say publicly must be reviewed by someone who does know, before it is made public.

ITT asserts that the company is not trying to put a muzzle on company officials; it is trying to ensure full and timely disclosure everywhere. For example, the manager in Berlin is free to propose the time and place to announce a plant expansion, but care must be taken to relay the information, i.e., to make it available to everyone else in the world who should have access to it. This is done most efficiently by turning it over to the corporate public affairs department.

To effect this centralized control, the company has an intricate but modestly staffed organization. Three area public relations directors outside the United States—one each in Europe, Latin America, and the Far East—are the conduits for the flow of information to corporate headquarters and the return of material approved for release. These persons have dual responsibilities and dual bosses. They are responsible for the total corporate relations and advertising function in their areas and, in this role, report to the area president. They are also responsible for compliance with corporate policy and procedures in the clearance and dissemination of information. In this capacity, they report to the director of corporate relations and advertising in New York.

At corporate headquarters, the director reports directly to the president and chief executive officer.

Included in the functions of the director's department, in addition to public affairs, press relations, and advertising, are corporate sales promotion, shows and exhibits, financial publications, annual reports, and corporate contributions. These activities are organized under a vice-president and deputy corporate director, a director of public relations, a director of advertising and sales promotion, and a director of the company's Washington office. In all, 36 people comprise the New York public affairs staff.

Public affairs gets top management attention

Public affairs policy is set and activities reviewed by the corporate Public Affairs Committee, and this is where the key pieces in the management mosaic come together.

Six persons are essentially in charge of ITT mainstream administration, and all six sit on the public affairs committee. In all there are ten members on the committee, including the director and deputy director of corporate relations and advertising. The president and chief executive officer is chairman of the public affairs committee.

Agendas for the quarterly meetings are made up by the corporate public affairs department. While specific current activities and issues make up a portion of every agenda, there are also items that look ahead. According to the deputy director, this committee is especially interested in how the company should conduct itself worldwide during the next few years.

That provides another insight into international public affairs. The function never matures and stabilizes. It is dynamic and volatile. It bears on problems that can seriously affect the company's operations. And it takes the best minds in the company to keep on top of the demands and challenges it presents.

5

Siemens AG

"A finger everywhere, a foot hardly anywhere"

World sales: $15.6 billion
Percent sales abroad: 50.5
Number of employees: 322,000
Countries with subsidiaries: 128
Central office: Federal Republic of Germany

Siemens AG has been a multinational operation since its inception in 1847. Today, about half its sales are from international business and 25 percent of its revenues derive from foreign sales of products manufactured in Germany. In short, 75 percent of its revenues are realized through its international operations.

The effectiveness of the company's international public affairs practices is indicated by the operating results from business in nearly 130 countries around the world. Annual sales volume has reached DM 20.7 billion. Profit on these operations in the fiscal year ending September 30, 1976, was DM 606 million.

The perennial hardiness of the company is indicated by the fact that it has been able to resume business as usual after the ravages of both world wars.

The company has grown to its present stature with relative smoothness and little public criticism. And it has done this during a time when national governments, upon which it depends heavily for its business, have undergone profound and frequently violent change.

The student of international public affairs must ask how this has been accomplished.

The terms "public relations" and "public affairs" do not appear in the organizational structure charts of Siemens. This does not mean that the company eschews these disciplines. On the contrary, it has virtually assimilated them into the management function. Command responsibility for public affairs rests with the manager in charge of the product group or company involved. Line responsibility—putting decision into practice—is directed by the same person, with certain tasks assigned to the appropriate staff department when its expertise and assistance are needed.

Local control

It is the operating manager's responsibility to identify and anticipate problems and develop a policy or approach to them. The operating manager does not formulate this approach without substantial assistance. Within the company he or she has rich resources to draw on.

An example is the recent economic and political turmoil in Portugal. Siemens executives there were aware of very active and well-organized forces opposing the Caetano Government. While the company remained carefully aloof, it was not taken by surprise when that government was overthrown in 1974. The company had monitored the situation closely throughout this period to determine the impact of events on operations.

Sales dropped substantially and the manufacturing facilities were underutilized. The new government would not allow the company to lay off workers or to introduce shorter work hours. Because of financial losses resulting from these government policies, some foreign companies closed their operations in Portugal. Siemens considered this, but decided against it.

The decision was based on a careful assessment of the situation by Siemens management in Portugal and specialists at headquarters in Munich. The assessment was that the upheaval eventually would stabilize. Siemens would be in a much better position at that point if the company remained in the country than it would be if it had to begin anew. Appropriate departments of the company informed interested parties of the decision to remain and Siemens rode out the storm. Subsequent events attest to the soundness of this management decision.

Following their own best judgment

Like troublesome issues, public criticism can be anticipated, but Siemens does not let the prospect of criticism influence decisions the company believes are sound. In 1972, Siemens became a major participant in the construction of the world's third largest dam, the Cabora Bassa in northern Mozambique. The dam would supply power for Mozambique, Rhodesia, and part of South Africa.

Mozambique at that time was a province of Portugal and along with Angola was the center of a worldwide controversy. Westinghouse Electric had planned to participate in the project but had withdrawn, partly at least because of pressure from anti-Portugese groups in the United States. Siemens anticipated similar pressure at home in Germany, especially from the leftist press and similar-leaning groups in German colleges and universities.

Management, however, was convinced that the long-range benefits of the dam to Africans outweighed the criticism the company would suffer. The decision was made to proceed. Management did not disregard the possibility of criticism, and a more active communications effort was mounted to deal with whatever developed.

Again, events demonstrated the soundness of the decision the company made. Mozambique has been given its independence. The now completed dam is one of the major resources of the new country. What critics feared has been proved wrong; just the opposite has been realized. Instead of shoring up colonial rule, the project is now benefiting a new nation.

Did Siemens anticipate this turn of events? No claim that it did has been forwarded, but, with the expertise the company brings to bear on such problems, it is highly probable that these developments were considered likely.

Policy versus approach

Siemens does not have a formal policy on public affairs. The company does, however, have policies that would appear to be dictated by practical public affairs considerations. For instance:

- From fiscal 1970 to 1976, foreign ownership of Siemens stock increased by from 20 to 30 percent. In view of the rising tide of nationalism, this seems a prudent move.

- Of the 97,000 employees of Siemens outside Germany, less than one percent are German nationals. There is strong representation of host nationals in executive positions in most foreign subsidiaries.

- The company avoids political involvement in host countries. Its representatives around the world are advised not to contribute to political parties or to get involved in national political activities.

- The company fosters the development of local technology, pays good wages, and helps train nationals of host countries employed in its branches "to climb the ladder of success."

- To help create a favorable world climate for multinational corporations, Siemens cooperated in formulating the guidelines for multinational companies recently released by the OECD and the

International Chamber of Commerce Code regarding foreign investment.

Altogether, these policies and actions imply a basic philosophy on public affairs, a pragmatic philosophy dictating actions that will best serve the advancement of the company as a whole.

Likewise, the company's approach to public affairs is pragmatic and undoubtedly based on its long experience in dealing with other countries. The company believes that, in most cases, foreign public affairs problems are as much a matter of personalities as they are of issues, that if one really understands the people and the policitians involved he or she can get an accurate reading of the situation and develop an effective solution to the problem.

Approach depends on sound Information

The success of this "people" approach to issues obviously depends on good information, gathered on the scene. And that is why the primary responsibility for Siemens international public affairs rests with local management.

These managers are not left to their own devices to deal with problems. Sensitivity to public affairs matters and the Siemens approach are cultivated throughout the course of a manager's development with the company. Close and frequent contact is maintained among all company executives around the world. Conferences are held in Munich every two or three years. Attending these conferences are all the top executives of the corporation, the heads of the seven major product groups, and all managers from companies worldwide.

At these conferences, review and discussion of public affairs case histories help formulate and clarify company philosophy and approaches. Committees are organized to study specific, evolving problems and to develop strategies that can be implemented when they return to their assigned posts.

The company's objective is to get all its managers on the same wavelength in the area of public affairs so they will be almost intuitively able to form judgments and guidelines consonant with company philosophy.

Staff support

The Siemens headquarters staff also provides substantial assistance for dealing with public affairs problems. When such a problem arises, the head of the company involved immediately contacts headquarters in

Munich by telephone or Telex. Once the problem is laid out, the appropriate headquarters resources are brought to bear. In dealing with a recent problem in Brazil, for instance, four persons prepared the recommended approach: the head of the Siemens company in Brazil, and three persons in Munich, namely, the top executive in the product group involved, an expert on Brazil from the Latin American desk, and a representative from the Central Information Department.

Once the basic approach is agreed to, the head of the unit concerned mobilizes the action. Functional units of the company are at his disposal to deal with virtually any contingency.

The key support group is the Central Information Department. Headed by a vice-president, this department is responsible for all press relations. The staff of 55 includes specialists for each major communications medium. For example, one senior staff member is responsible for contacts with all daily newspapers. This person has extensive prior experience with the press. Another senior staffer is responsible for all information given to economic media and has prior business-press experience. There are similar experts for each type of communications medium.

The Central Information Department also monitors news sources for information about activities that could affect Siemens' operations. This information is reported to the appropriate product group or company manager.

Staff departments share responsiblity

In dealing with public affairs problems, the second functional unit most frequently called upon is the advertising department. When directed to do so, this department can develop and place public affairs support advertising virtually anywhere in the world. It is also responsible for brochures, expositions, and trade shows, any of which can be used to advance Siemens' position on public issues.

The central personnel division may also play a role. This unit is responsible for publications and communications to more than 300,000 Siemens employees around the world.

When the public affairs situation may be of concern to stockholders, the finance division is called upon to handle the necessary communications to that particular audience.

If a problem involves government relations, it is quite possible that members of the managing board itself, or at least one member of it, will act as the liaison with whatever government people or agencies are concerned.

To close the circuit with all these functional units, each product group director has at least one information specialist on his staff. It is this person's responsibility to work with Central Information and any other unit concerned in preparing product group material for release.

The net result is a system totally and completely integrated into the management function. The system gathers information, evaluates its potential impact on the company, determines policy or approach based on experience and seasoned judgment, and then takes the actions dictated.

The achievements of this system were aptly summarized in a detailed company profile published in *The Economist:* "Siemens pursues an international strategy of diversification and achieves it without attracting undesirable attention to itself—political or otherwise."

One board member is reputed to have put it more succinctly: "A finger everywhere, a foot hardly anywhere."

6

Citibank, N.A.

"A requirement for public affairs consciousness"

Worldwide assets: $87 billion
Percent assets from abroad: 64
Number of employees: 48,000
Number of offices abroad: 92
Central office: United States

Citibank, N.A., principal subsidiary of Citicorp, is a full-service commercial bank serving consumers, business and financial institutions, and governments throughout the world. In 1975, for the first time, its overseas operations in 103 countries outstripped domestic operations in all three categories of financial performance—loans, deposits, and net interest revenue. (Foreign deposits had passed domestic deposits in 1974.)

Over the past five years, working against a corporate goal of 15 percent earnings increase per year, overseas operations and revenues have grown more rapidly than the domestic. The 15 percent target is retained, which means continued expansion overseas.

Citibank's operating philosophy has proved successful. It is simply stated. The bank believes it must gear its operations in any country to the economic aspirations of the local citizens. In most countries, this means a close study of government economic planning, then aligning the bank's operations to help achieve appropriate objectives within these national plans.

The job of public affairs is to help keep this basic approach on track and to provide continuous communication of the effort to appropriate publics within the host country.

Because Citibank customizes its services to the needs of the host country, its overseas operations are almost perforce decentralized, autonomous profit centers, country by country. It follows that the public affairs program must be customized country by country as well. Public affairs in each country, then, comes under the autonomy of the bank manager in the country.

47

Responsibilities

The bank's senior officer in each country is responsible for public affairs in that country, just as he or she is for profit performance. In the over-all operating structure, a corporate administrative function for public affairs sets standards; provides training, guidance, and professional back-up assistance as required; and evaluates results. Responsibility for this corporate function rests with the director of international public affairs in New York.

He describes his responsibilities this way: ". . . managing the relations between the bank's policies and public opinion around the world to foster an atmosphere where we can do business profitably by telling people what we can do, in any honest way. To accomplish this requires more than counseling senior management and managing daily public affairs activities in New York. It requires establishing public affairs policies and capacities—and a public affairs consciousness—among all levels of management throughout our operations in the United States and abroad."

Awareness and capability

Two concepts stand out in this description. Both are given as requirements for accomplishing the job. One is establishing a public affairs capacity. The other is establishing a public affairs *consciousness*. These are given as worldwide goals—requirements—not as accomplished facts.

A third goal has to do with the caliber of public relations provided. The objective of the public affairs department is to run operations of the same high caliber in all locations. Criteria are ethical standards ("keeping everything aboveboard") and presenting common and consistent views on topics central to the bank's worldwide operations. These include such subjects as free trade, foreign branch banking, floating exchange rates, and the role of the multinational in world development.

Organization

Citibank's international public affairs program is organized as a service function readily available to any operating entity. The bank has four regional headquarters for its worldwide operations, and a regional public affairs director is assigned to each. This regional director is responsible for public affairs activities in all countries in the region. Each regional director has one assistant. These people report to the international public affairs director in New York.

The regional director visits the countries in his or her area periodically, briefs each country's senior officer and public affairs officer on pertinent developments, and issues and provides guidance and assistance as required. Senior officers and their public affairs officers in each country are expected to check with their regional director or with the international public affairs director when a question arises about the appropriateness of their actions.

The regional directors and the international director can challenge local initiatives. Moreover, they have veto power over local decisions when such decisions have serious public affairs implications. If a satisfactory solution cannot be reached between the country senior officer and the public affairs department, the matter can be referred to Citibank's chairman and chief executive officer for a final decision.

The autonomous profit centers are encouraged to use corporate public affairs services in three ways: by policy requirements, by personal contact and assistance initiated by regional public affairs directors, and by informational and training programs at corporate headquarters.

Policy

The Citibank corporate policy manual states that, wherever feasible, contact with the press must be cleared through or reported to the public affairs department. In practice, it is necessary to extend this rule beyond contacts with the press to advertising and other communications to the public. This policy is intended to coordinate communications so that public presentation of bank policy and positions is consistent.

In 1976, an additional policy was introduced. Each manager's annual operating plan must now include a public affairs plan. This plan is quite detailed and geared to the bank's objectives or business plan in the country concerned. Specifications for the plan call for six sections:

1. Description of the environment in which the bank operates.
2. Identification of target publics that may affect the bank.
3. Specific objectives to be achieved with each public.
4. Action programs to achieve these objectives.
5. Staff requirements and budget.
6. An evaluation component, conducted semiannually.

Many national plans address Citibank's image in the individual country with the bank focusing on unfavorable elements connected with its size (it is often the largest foreign bank in the country), its foreignness, and its aggressiveness. On the positive side, the company stresses the employment of local nationals in top positions and its contributions to the host country. National public affairs plans must be approved by the senior bank officer in a given country and included in the total operating plan. This makes public affairs an integral part of the senior executive's job in each country.

Personal contact

The primary responsibility of the regional public affairs director is to work with and assist the people responsible for public affairs in the countries within his or her area. The regional directors and their assistants do not wait to be called upon. They actively initiate involvement.

The level of involvement varies from country to country. In 14 countries, a full-time public affairs officer has been appointed by and reports to the country senior officer. In 35 countries, a staff person has a specific assignment, though not full-time, for public affairs. In the balance of the countries, public affairs are handled by the senior officer.

The business plan for each country is the basic starting point for the regional public affairs director. With this information about operations in the country, he or she can identify trends, events, policies, and other circumstances outside the country that can affect these operations. Information on such matters forms the basis for the briefing sessions when the regional public affairs director visits individual countries in his or her region.

Based on the briefing sessions, specific activities may be agreed upon. If local staff is available, action is taken internally; if not, the regional director or an assistant will take on the assignment.

Regional directors also become involved in the annual public affairs plan for each country. In some countries, they actually write the plan. In others, where staff is assigned, they provide counsel and guidance. They also participate in the semiannual plan reviews and evaluation of results.

The basic objective of these personal contacts is not simply to make things happen; there is a longer-range objective. That is to raise the level of awareness of bank operating personnel of the public affairs implications of their actions. If they are not aware that an action can have public affairs implications, they are not likely to check it out before acting. This is one of the major causes of internally generated public affairs problems.

Training

Sensitizing bank operating personnel to the public affairs implications of actions and training them to deal with public affairs problems are primary concerns of the corporate public affairs staff at New York headquarters.

The task is not easy. There is much more incentive for managers to achieve earnings growth of 15 percent per year than for them to run a successful public affairs program. As a consequence, when conflicts between these two objectives arise, as they inevitably do, the profit objective usually prevails.

Added to the problem of motivation is the more basic problem of awareness. New employees for line assignments have little or no training in public affairs. Most are business school graduates, and the corporate public affairs staff finds "their historical, political, and social awareness generally low. They have limited exposure to broad societal trends and the views of critics. For instance, very few have any familiarity with liberal or radical publications."

No specific public affairs ingredient is given in the initial training these people receive from the bank. Then they move rapidly into line assignments with strong pressure for high earnings performance. The public affairs aspects of operations are learned on the firing line.

To upgrade public affairs performance, the bank has arranged with a university communications department for a special six-week course. This course is attended by bank public affairs officers from abroad as well as from the United States.

Another effort at elevating awareness is a quarterly summary of public affairs problems, activities, and local policies. This document is published in New York and sent to all public affairs officers, domestic and foreign. Additional communications in this vein are being investigated.

Conferences for regional and local public affairs officers worldwide are held semiannually. The agenda are heavily oriented to problem solving. Three or four public affairs problems are studied and discussed in depth. The problems may be selected for their broad implications or because they are typical local problems everyone will face at one time or another. Each problem is posed to the attendees and they work out solutions and plans of action.

These problems and, indeed, actions in public affairs programs around the world, are not always negative or defensive. Many entail affirmative efforts to build understanding and goodwill and to head off problems before they occur.

The organization at work

A few examples of programs at work illustrate this better than the agenda of training seminars:

Citibank has technical expertise in business and money management. Through programs in a number of countries, the company shares this technology with the local business and banking community. Regular training sessions are held on the bank's premises. Local participants are businesspeople, including people working for competitive banks. The result is an upgrading of the business expertise of the entire community.

In Taiwan, the bank's guest observer program sends individuals from local government agencies and commercial banks to the United States for special three and six month training sessions.

There is obvious efficiency in a decentralized public affairs structure. Citibank operates with an overseas corporate staff of just eight professionals. But there are problems as well. A consciousness of and capacity for public affairs within the profit centers are essential. Internally generated problems can almost always be traced to a shortcoming in one or the other. While this kind of operation may have a higher incidence of internally generated problems than a tightly controlled, centralized operation, it would be hard to say that such problems have slowed the growth of Citibank overseas.

These problems could perhaps be reduced with more stringent corporate controls, which could be introduced without compromising the profit center structure. For instance, public affairs performance as well as profit performance could be introduced as criteria for evaluating and rating the performance of profit center managers. But, even without this, there is a dynamism in this kind of structure that works, a dynamism to which even the problems contribute in generating continually rising levels of competence. Problems motivate the profit center to improve and avoid recurrence. The corporate public affairs department is always there to help.

Part Three

How products and services affect public affairs

The influence of a company's products on the public affairs function is illustrated in our case studies of Ericsson and Renault. Ericsson's main product, telecommunications equipment, is a sensitive one. Telecommunications is both a critical and an expensive public service in a country. Because it is especially sensitive to a country's security and prosperity, government involvement is almost guaranteed on this count alone. When one considers the magnitude of investment required for a modern telecommunications system, the inevitability of government involvement is again apparent. In most countries, the government is the only institution capable of raising the kind of investment capital needed. The impact of both these influences is clearly evident in the Ericsson case history.

Automobiles are also important to a country's development. A country that does not have a strong domestic industry is frequently eager to develop one. Where a country has a domestic automobile industry, the government is not always open to sharing domestic markets of this magnitude with foreign manufacturers. Renault is well aware of the public affairs implications of its products and has a direct way of dealing with resulting situations.

7

L. M. Ericsson Telephone Company

"First, control the technology."

World sales: $1.7 billion
Percent sales abroad: 85
Number of employees: 70,000
Countries with subsidiaries: 69
Central office: Sweden

Telecommunications is a crucial element in both the economic and political structures of a country. The public telephone exchange is a key control point. Many a government believes its country's telecommunications systems are too important to be in private hands. This is especially true if the private hands are from a foreign country.

The business of L. M. Ericsson Telephone Company with headquarters in Sweden puts it face to face with all the ramifications of these sensitive issues. The company is in telecommunications and nearly half of its sales are in public telephone exchanges. In more than 100 countries around the world, where it does 85 percent of its business, Ericsson is in such a position: it is a "foreign" company.

Dealing with these sensitivities is complicated by another factor. The telecommunications business is highly capital intensive. It takes a lot of money to build and install a telecommunications system. If a company is to handle such contracts, it must have access to very substantial amounts of capital. That means it must be well known and respected in the world financial community.

The interrelationships of these factors have a fundamental influence on the public affairs policy of Ericsson. The company must walk a fine line to maintain a proper balance between the requirements imposed by the sensitivities of its major customers—foreign governments—and the need to instill and hold the confidence of the international financial community.

Subsidiaries concentrate on local needs

Ericsson does this in part by separating the corporate and subsidiary functions. The subsidiary is concerned with creating a favorable business climate in the host country. The corporation provides support as needed and is concerned with internatonal matters, especially those relating to international finance.

This does not mean the corporation maintains a hands-off policy toward its subsidiaries when it comes to public affairs matters. On the contrary, corporate policy sets the tone, and, at times, corporate people become deeply involved in specific problems. But actions are taken through the local manager.

In any given country, the Ericsson subsidiary tries to keep a low public posture. This is dictated by the market the company serves. Only a few people in any country have decision-making power on the purchase of telecommunications systems. So there is no marketing need for broad public recognition of the company.

Indeed, broad public recognition could be a marketing problem rather than a help. Most decision makers in the purchase of telecommunications systems are government officials. Spending large sums with a foreign company is never politically popular. Thus a low level of public recognition of Ericsson as a multinational corporation is much more advantageous.

These political overtones also make it expedient for Ericsson subsidiaries to assume the posture of a local company, so far as is possible. For this reason, the country manager, not Swedish headquarters, is the corporation in that country.

To back up the individual country manager, Ericsson will readily build a manufacturing facility in a country with enough business. In this way, a significant proportion of the equipment sold in that country will be manufactured there. As a result of this policy, Ericsson has 35 manufacturing subsidiaries in 15 countries and nonmanufacturing subsidiaries in 50 countries. Collectively these international subsidiaries employ 40,000 people. At home in Sweden, by comparison, Ericsson employs 30,000 people.

At corporate headquarters, public affairs and advertising are under the direction of a vice-president who is a member of the management group and reports to the president. This office coordinates public affairs and advertising activities around the world and handles all shareholder communications and financial community relations worldwide. The annual report, produced in three languages, is prepared in this office as are periodic announcements of financially significant occurrences.

Dealing with public affairs problems

One of the most pressing public affairs problems Ericsson faces, its management reports, is nationalism. The company sees a mounting worldwide trend in this direction. And the telecommunications industry is a likely target when nationalization becomes an active program in a country. Ericsson's policy on this issue is pragmatic. The company's management believes that the best insurance against nationalization is shared ownership, either with the government of the host country or with private investors there. And the company takes out a lot of this kind of insurance.

Ericsson prefers to hold more than 50 percent ownership, but this is not always possible. The company can sometimes maintain control, however, even with minority equity. It does this with licensing agreements. The company owns the technology that makes its systems work, so the licensing agreements have a great deal of leverage.

Nationalism isn't all bad

Ericsson has demonstrated that even nationalistic trends can be turned to advantage when one controls the technology. In 1975, the French government adopted a policy that key industries would be French owned. The telecommunications industry was high on the list of key industries. In negotiations with the government, Ericsson reached an agreement whereby it sold 65 percent of its operations in France to French interests and retained 35 percent.

These negotiations were conducted without publicity. No announcements were made until the final agreement was consummated. At that time, announcement of amicable and satisfactory agreement was made in France. Employees and shareholders around the world were notified of the transaction by communications from corporate headquarters.

While Ericsson's French arrangement probably raised some eyebrows around the world, it appears to have worked out well for Ericsson. The company's sales in France rose to more than $200 million in 1976, making France Ericsson's second largest single customer outside Sweden. The increased purchases in France, of course, were for high technology components that Ericsson makes only in Sweden.

Labor relations as public affairs

The labor movement in Europe poses the second most important public affairs problem, in the view of Ericsson management. It is closely tied to the issue of nationalism. Ericsson management sees a well-organized effort by leftist union leaders that, if successful, could unduly restrict and seriously impede the operations of multinational corporations.

The issue raised by unions is that multinationals take jobs out of the country. Unions are asking for measures that would determine when this was happening and authority to stop it.

This argument works against multinationals both at home and in every country where they sell imported goods. Unions at home don't want the company to export, and unions in the host country don't want the company to import. Two factors make it a particularly tough argument to rebut. First it has strong appeal based on fear of losing jobs. Second, an effective rebuttal is so complicated that it is difficult to convey.

Ericsson is making a concerted effort in Sweden to deliver this rebuttal in person to union leaders and at various seats of learning where the concept has currency. The question it must answer in Sweden is: "Why are 60 percent of the company's workers employed outside Sweden?" It tries to answer by pointing out that 86 percent of its sales come from outside Sweden, so its foreign business is creating jobs at home that wouldn't exist if it did not operate in international markets.

Making the most of company strengths

Ericsson strikes a fine balance in its worldwide operations. It gives where it must. But the company holds a technological edge that ensures a substantial and growing segment of the market. There are only a handful of companies in the world that have the technology and resources to build and service a modern telecommunications system. Ericsson is one. If a country needs a modern system, Ericsson will be in the running to provide it.

The company carefully cultivates and nurtures its strengths. It has a strong base of support in the financial community with 130,000 shareholders around the world. It serves these people well, and this practice gives the company the financial resources it needs.

The company's technology base is maintained essentially in Sweden. Ericsson invests handsomely in research and development to keep this key resource current and viable in a very competitive field.

The company has still another vital resource in Sweden—its highly skilled labor force. With this extremely valuable labor pool, built up over many years, Ericsson has the capability to manufacture the more sophisticated components for its system at home, where it has full control.

This control of the technology gives Ericsson ultimate control over its destiny abroad. It can seemingly sell out, as it did in France, and end up doing more business than before. Its public affairs efforts are aimed at creating the climate in which this can continue to happen.

8

Renault

"A Latin style of operation"

World sales: $13 billion
Percent sales abroad: 45
Number of employees: 243,000
Countries with subsidiaries: 34
Central office: France

Renault is 94 percent owned by the French government, but the company operates as a competitive entity in the private sector. The company is not subsidized as a national monopoly, as railroads or postal services might be. Indeed, the French government, like any other shareholder, expects Renault to produce a profit. The major difference is the way the government uses the profits. Mainly they are plowed back into expansion to create more jobs—the bottom line on the political ledger.

Government ownership and the political ledger it implies have a decided impact on Renault's public affairs practices in France. But outside France, the company maintains, the government does not become involved in Renault's operations any more than it would for a privately owned French company. Company executives insist that the government does not intercede for Renault or negotiate business agreements with other countries. These negotiations are handled by Renault officials, just as they would be under private ownership.

No matter how carefully Renault and the French government separate these matters, however, it is difficult to imagine that the distinction is fully recognized by host countries. It would be hard for a host country faced with sensitive decisions not to take into account the fact that the company is owned by the French government.

Ownership, obviously, has had no adverse effect on the company. Renault is a major multinational. The company produces 1.6 million vehicles a year. Nearly 56 percent are sold outside France. Renault operates factories and assembly plants in 27 countries. The company currently has some 14,000 dealerships; 7,600, or more than half, are outside France.

With France's membership in the EEC, most of Europe is virtually a domestic market for Renault. Production facilities for this market are located in France, creating 160,000 jobs for French workers. Foreign operations serve other major markets.

Emphasis on problem prevention

In its foreign operations, Renault's basic international public affairs approach seems to avert serious difficulty by settling problems in advance with the host government. These negotiations are handled by Renault's international affairs department, and they appear to be aimed at putting operations in the host country on a sound footing at the beginning.

A strong indication of this approach is found in the pattern of ownership of overseas Renault operations. In each country, ownership appears to be resolved in terms of the host country's national objectives. In Spain, Renault owns 50 percent of the company, a major facility; the balance is owned by Spanish banks. In Colombia, half the company is owned by Renault and half by the Colombian government.

In communist countries, virtually no foreign ownership is permitted. So Renault operates under licensing contracts. The company sells its technology, tools, and patterns to the government corporation. This frequently entails building an entire plant. The government corporation then takes over and manufactures and distributes Renault vehicles. Renault has such arrangements in Rumania, Yugoslavia, Poland, and the Soviet Union.

These are not unusual arrangements. Many other multinational corporations have similar ones. But there has been some controversy over such solutions in France. A leading auto industry economist in Paris has criticized the Renault policy of building foreign plants rather than exporting vehicles made domestically. He maintains this policy is based on political rather than economic reasoning and will offer only a "few crumbs" compared to the profit margin that might be attained on exported vehicles.

Response by the chairman of Renault was couched in business terms. He claims there are handsome profits to be made from building plants for foreign governments. And he maintains that Renault must do it this way or lose the market entirely.

Public awareness of company is high

Being owned by the government and at the same time being one of the country's largest employers, Renault is very much in the public eye at home. And it is here that the company concentrates its greatest efforts in public affairs. When the company becomes embroiled in controversy, as in the instance cited, the chief executive is usually the spokesperson who deals with it.

The basis for dealing with controversy is the social benefit for the French as frequently as it is sound business practice. In its position, the company is almost compelled to be socially minded. Indeed, Renault executives believe that in France a reputation for social-mindedness is as important as a reputation for high-quality cars. In gaining this reputation, the company has been a pioneer in social causes. The French workers' movement started at Renault. The company was the first in the country to provide three and then four weeks of vacation. Renault is also responsible for another innovation considered a social advantage—paying workers on a monthly rather than weekly basis.

The company's public relations department is in the office of the chief executive officer, and its primary emphasis is on France. One group in the department deals with product publicity and exhibits. Another specializes in working with the economic and trade press. The third concentrates on government relations and, through the national auto industry association, on matters concerning the industry.

Market effect guides decisions

The department is available to help overseas operations, but the responsibility is delegated to the subsidiary. There is one guideline: decisions on public affairs matters should be made on the basis of what will most help (or least harm) the sale of Renault cars and trucks.

Executives of the company maintain it is organized on the Latin rather than the Anglo-Saxon tradition. It operates much like privately owned companies in France, Italy, and Spain. The chief executive is the person who makes the decisions and addresses the public. The company organization is flexible, and there are no complicated lines of who reports to whom. Everyone adjusts to implement the decisions of the chief executive officer.

It follows that there is very little in writing relating to policy. Policy is determined by the chief executive. When this is done and the direction is set, instructions on implementation are put in writing.

Management directors of overseas operations work much the same way within their operations and have a lot of flexibility on reporting and clearing actions with Paris.

No assistance from government

In all of this, there is very little interplay with or reliance on the French government. In the spring of 1976, for example, a major crisis occurred in Argentina. The manager of one of the two Renault plants there was killed by terrorists. No decisions or actions were taken in Paris either by Renault or by the French government. All actions and communications with the press and any decisions or protests to be made to the government of Argentina were made through the Renault managing director in Argentina.

The assessment was made that this was an isolated incident directed at all foreign companies rather than Renault in particular, and the situation was handled on that basis.

Conceivably, Renault executives say, the French government might step in and use its influence in a public affairs problem in another country but only under circumstances that would call for government action even if the company were privately owned. Such an occasion might arise, for instance, if a foreign government tried to hold down the price of Renault cars and trucks sold in that country to the point where profit would be eliminated and the plant in the country forced to close.

In such a case, Renault officials say, company executives would contact the host government to find out how serious the situation actually was. Is the measure being seriously considered, or is it a gesture being made for political reasons with no intention of being implemented?

If the threats were real, company officials would point out "directly and dramatically" to the foreign government that if the measure were put into effect, Renault would be forced to close down its plant. If all preliminary measures failed, the French government's commercial advisor might intercede to reinforce the company's view, just as it would for any other French-based company.

Based on this hypothetical example, it would appear that, when the question arises of *whether* Renault operates in a country, the French government becomes involved. If it is a question of *how* Renault operates in the country, it is solely up to the country.

Renault apppears to have a single, simple approach to international public affairs: a preemptive strategy implemented through direct advance negotiations with the host government. The company is working toward the same goal as its sister multinationals—creating an atmosphere conducive to the conduct of its business.

Part Four

How marketing interfaces affect public affairs

The differing effects of marketing interfaces on the public affairs function are illustrated in the ASEA and Mobil cases. Potential buyers of ASEA's power-generating equipment and electrical products are few and easily identified. Frequently these buyers are found in government, and this poses problems typical of those encountered by those multinational corporations which make large sales contracts with foreign governments. These problems have a major influence on the shape of the company's public affairs function.

At Mobil, the marketing interface is as broad as the one at ASEA is narrow. Mobil sells petroleum products across the board—to the public, to industrial users and to governments. The oil embargo precipitated a new era that heightened the importance of these interfaces on public affairs practices and activities in the company's overseas operations.

9

ASEA

"Expand where public affairs problems are manageable."

World sales: $2.3 billion
Percent sales abroad: 54
Number of employees: 43,000
Countries with subsidiaries: 35
Central office: Sweden

ASEA is a major Swedish manufacturer of heavy industrial equipment. About 40 percent of its sales are in power-generating and transmission equipment, and almost half of these (or 21 percent of total sales) are in nuclear reactors.

In the United States, that alone would imply enough public affairs problems to last a lifetime. On the world market, ASEA has not found this to be a special problem.

While ASEA has always sold some goods abroad, the company did not place major emphasis on overseas business until the late 1960s. Even then, ASEA did not enter the international scene with visions of becoming a giant multinational corporation. Rather, management says, the decision was thrust upon the company by circumstances.

Dr. Marcus Wallenberg, honorary chairman, explains it this way: "If we don't compete in other markets with foreign companies who are competing with us in Sweden, we can certainly never defend our Swedish market."

Dr. Curt Nicolin, ASEA group chairman, explains the decision from a different perspective. Until the end of the 1950s, he says, demand for ASEA products in Sweden alone required a steadily increasing number of employees. In the late 1960s, however, this demand stabilized. Projections showed that domestic demand in the future could be met with a declining number of employees. If current Swedish employment were to be maintained, he concluded, it would be necessary to increase foreign sales.

By either account, the move into foreign markets was essentially a defensive measure. Nevertheless the company pursued its decision aggressively.

Between 1960 and 1970, ASEA's total employment remained almost constant, but the work assignment ratios of employees changed dramatically. The number of those engaged in production for foreign markets more than doubled, the increase almost equaling the loss in those employed in production for the Swedish market. By 1970, while the total number of employees was about equal to that in 1960, employment was almost equally divided between production for domestic and foreign markets.

All of this, of course, reflected changes that had taken place in the company's sales. Overseas sales had grown to match domestic sales. Since 1970, this ratio has remained fairly constant.

ASEA has good reason to be pleased with the results it has realized with the fifty-fifty ratio. Between 1971 and 1975, sales doubled, both in Sweden and in world markets. Profits rose from $1.85 to $6.70 per share. And employment, after remaining on a plateau for nearly a decade, climbed substantially.

Reorganizing to consolidate gains

Thus ASEA has passed through a significant transition in the past 15 years. And the company was recently reorganized to deal more effectively with the opportunities inherent in its new multinational character and its technological leadership in a broad range of applications.

As part of this reorganization, the ASEA Group was formed to plan and coordinate activities of all ASEA companies. The group functions not unlike a holding company but also conducts some corporate operations. Here the policy and planning functions for the ASEA family of companies now rest. High on the list of duties for the group's executive officers is the framing of a long-term strategic plan for the total company. Reporting to the chairman are the staff officers necessary for this: group officials responsible for corporate finance and accounting, corporate counsel, corporate auditing, and a division called corporate environment.

The public affairs organization

Corporate environment is the new designation for what was previously called public affairs. The director is a vice-president and member of the ASEA management group. Prior to reorganization, the director was head of public affairs. While the new designation is intended to reflect the company's strong concern for environment in the commonly accepted use of the term, ASEA executives also view the function as encompassing "political, trade, and press environment" as well.

It is the responsibility of the corporate environment director to advise the president and chief executive officer on current public affairs problems and to apprise them of environmental trends that might become important to the company. This emphasis on anticipating problems is not new with ASEA. The corporate environment department in the new organization is viewed more accurately as a natural evolution of past practices. Such practices, the company says, have been quite successful.

The corporate environment director says ASEA currently does not face really significant public affairs problems. This is due, at least in part, he contends, to the fact that ASEA management tries to put its emphasis on expansion and product promotion in parts of the world where it is believed public affairs problems are of a manageable nature.

Anticipating problems and opportunities

The corporate environment department carries on this anticipatory function. The department compiles and assesses data obtained through its own research and from reports submitted by ASEA managers and consultants around the world. It regularly issues "strategic orientation" documents based on these studies. These papers spotlight political and social problems around the world and their likely impact on ASEA. Some documents summarize and provide advice on decisions by OECD, EEC, and other supranational organizations.

These orientation documents are circulated for decision-making guidance to a small group of executives in Sweden and abroad. The documents also are critical for the company's strategic plan and for establishing yearly management and public affairs objectives.

Use of outside counsel

The corporate environment department staff concentrates on broad issues and trends and hires outside assistance when specific expertise is required for solving a problem. When the company was charged with selling products in the United States below prevailing market price, it retained U.S. public relations counsel. The reasons: the U.S. firm was more familiar with the complex political, economic, and media relationships involved in the charges than was ASEA management. Likewise in Great Britain, Greece, Germany, and Japan, where ASEA management has encountered or anticipated problems or opportunities peculiar to the individual country, special advisors have been retained.

Information programs undertaken by ASEA staff, like the company's policy and planning, are addressed to broad issues. The company is very well known in Sweden. Outside of Sweden, it is not so well known. If ASEA is to expand in international markets, this situation is not entirely desirable. This is a need that the company is addressing aggressively.

It is not difficult for ASEA to pinpoint target audiences or to determine the messages to be conveyed. ASEA wants to expand its world markets. In each country the market for the company's equipment is small, highly sophisticated, and readily identifiable. Primarily, the company wants to be known in the private sector to top executives and design engineers in the electric power, transmission, transportation, and high-technology industries. In the public sector, the target audience consists of government officials and bureaucrats with official duties in these areas. However, because the company realizes the importance of public approval when selling to government, it aggressively seeks public recognition as well.

The growing importance of identity

ASEA sees two trends that make its reputation within the public sector more important than ever before. The first is the growing trend toward protectionism, especially where major investments are concerned. The second is ASEA's increasing activity in atomic reactors and electrical transmission.

ASEA has clearly specified the messages to be conveyed to its target audiences:

- Breadth and technical quality of electrical products—better than those produced locally in most countries.
- International scope of products and services with emphasis on training local technicians and executives in the use of ASEA technology.
- Responsibility in management and research with emphasis on environmental protection and safety measures, especially in the field of nuclear reactors and nuclear waste disposal.

These messages are conveyed and emphasized in all company communications: advertising, press releases, internal and external publications, and speeches by executives at company-sponsored events.

Use of company publications

Company publications are used extensively in this effort. An annual publication, *ASEA Today*, is issued solely for this purpose. The publication describes technical developments by ASEA. It is printed in 11 languages, including English, Russian, Chinese, and Japanese. Copies are sent to "anyone who is a potential customer or who might influence a customer."

Another publication, *ASEA International,* is a quarterly journal dealing mainly with the relationship between society and technology. The journal is distributed to opinion leaders under the name of the top ASEA executive in the particular country.

The annual report, which gets broad international distribution, is also part of this effort. In addition to the required financial information, the report regularly contains a discussion by a top executive of some aspect of one of the basic messages. The full report and summaries are printed in Swedish and English; summaries also are printed in German, French, Spanish, and Italian.

A maturing function

Like the company's international business, ASEA's public affairs program is maturing and taking on characteristics noted in more seasoned multinationals. Heavy emphasis is placed on anticipating problems. Important group influences are identified and efforts are made to communicate with them. Problems are dealt with by experts in the country where the problems occur.

While ASEA has done well with its approach, the company recognizes that in today's climate major challenges may arise at any time. ASEA will inevitably be involved with the governments of host countries, because those governments are making more decisions on purchases and installations of the types of products ASEA manufactures and sells. This involvement adds a new dimension to the buy-and-sell negotiations that customarily take place between companies.

ASEA is introducing itself currently to these people in the public sector through its communications. Such introductory communications play up the company's strong suit—advanced technology—the technology the host country presumably needs and may not have. And this strength, it would seem, will be the basis for the public affairs strategy ASEA will follow at this more complicated level of international trade.

10

Mobil Oil Corporation

"Public affairs is a line responsibility."

World sales: $26.2 billion
Percent sales abroad: 67
Number of employees: 71,000
Countries with subsidiaries: 75+
Central office: United States

In practice, the public affairs function involves the line manager in most situations. At Mobil Oil, policy makes public affairs the line manager's responsibility and the function is clearly organized along these lines.

Mobil Oil Corporation is a fully integrated oil company. That is, it has crude oil production, transportation, refining, and marketing interests. These interests span the globe with marketing the most widespread. Mobil products are sold in more than 100 countries. Worldwide, the Mobil Oil organization employs 71,000 people.

Mobil's worldwide organization is built with affiliate companies. For the most part, affiliates are in charge of all Mobil business in a single country. The three largest foreign affiliates—in Germany, Japan, and South Africa—coordinate their activities directly with Mobil's International Division in New York. The others coordinate their activities with one of the regional service companies around the world, and these regional service companies then coordinate activities with the International Division.

Each affiliate manager is responsible for public affairs in his or her area. At headquarters in New York, a coordinator within the corporate public relations department serving the International Division provides back-up services, advice, and counsel. But the decisions are made by the affiliate.

Germany and the oil crisis

The following example shows how this works in practice. The 1973 oil crisis hit Germany much as it did the United States. Warnings had gone unheeded and most Germans assumed low cost energy would continue to be abundant. The oil shortage provided a rude shock. As in the United States, the oil companies were held largely to blame.

The general manager of Mobil's affiliate in Germany decided to take the initiative in explaining the crisis. Under his direction, a four-stage communications program was planned.

First, a detailed explanation of the situation was prepared for employees. This material covered the cost of importing crude and an explanation of the role of profits in financing new oil and gas reserves. As the oil companies were blamed for making undue profits during the crisis, cost/revenue calculations were issued explaining the impact of OPEC price increases on product prices. Also covered were "inventory profits." Employees were urged to pass this information along to friends and associates when questions were raised about the problem.

The second step was a mail campaign to major customers and distributors. Information similar to that communicated to employees was tailored specifically to customer and distributor questions and problems.

In the third stage, the German affiliate elected not to use institutional advertising to reach the public at large. Instead, a series of billboards and brochures were developed and arranged to be displayed and distributed through savings banks. The illustrations depicted the various activities connected with finding, producing, refining, and marketing oil-based energy. A brochure containing the same type of information was prepared and distributed free at the displays in the banks. The banks enthusiastically supported this effort because the posters were attractive, the brochures informative, and the subject matter of keen interest to the public. Banks helped promote the exhibits. To stimulate even greater interest, people were given questions at the exhibits and invited to write their answers and comments to the German affiliate headquarters. Prizes were offered. The company received 30,000 replies. The bank exhibits were so well received that the affiliate also offered them to schools. This offer met with equal success.

A press effort was the fourth stage of this campaign. The announcement and unveiling of the posters provided an opportunity to gain national publicity. The opening of each poster display in a bank offered additional opportunity for local publicity. A discussion of the posters with reporters provided an ideal opportunity for review of Mobil's points and positions.

This entire campaign was designed, researched, developed, and carried out by the German affiliate. Material developed in New York for Mobil's campaign in the United States was reviewed for ideas and some staff work was supplied by New York people.

Corporate staff sets tone

The function of the staff at Mobil's New York headquarters is to ensure, so far as possible, that the Mobil companies "speak with one voice, worldwide." The staff sets the tone with a highly developed program in the United States and provides guidance and direction for the affiliates. Headquarters only becomes involved when the affiliate requests help or when the issue spills over national boundaries and involves other countries.

In this kind of decentralized function, "speaking with one voice worldwide" is no small task. The organization works at this activity at both the policy-making level and the operational level.

The Mobil companies' position on key issues is determined at the very top. The chairman of the board of the parent corporation takes ultimate responsibility. Support responsibility is clearly vested in affiliate managers. They are responsible for seeing that organization policy is followed in their operations and for setting policy on local issues. An affiliate's policy is expected to reflect the spirit of corporate policy.

Communication's policy

The most important means of conveying the spirit and the letter of this policy is the annual affiliate managers' conference. Each year the general managers of the affiliates meet for review and coordination of organization goals and objectives. Public affairs is usually one of the major topics of discussion. The Mobil companies have found that this kind of discussion develops better understanding and application of policy than written codes or policy guidelines. Broad policy, therefore, is not written.

Subsequent to the affiliate managers' conference as specific issues or problems arise concerning the organization, policy guidance is determined by top corporate management and conveyed to those affiliate managers concerned or affected. This is done by personal visits, telephone, Telex, or internal mail, depending on the urgency of the situation and the number of affiliate managers affected. At the operational level, corporate and affiliate staff functions make this work. Corporate staff persons are available to affiliates for consultation and policy guidance when a question arises on policy in general or on a specific issue. In addition, the annual public affairs program prepared by each affiliate is reviewed by corporate staff to ensure that the objectives and aims of the programs conform to corporation policy. As a final check, corporate staff conducts periodic audits of activities conducted in connection with affiliate programs.

Implementation follows policy

Implementing programs, as noted in the case of the German affiliate, is entirely the responsibility of the affiliate. Affiliate budgets and staffs for these activities vary according to their needs. The German affiliate, for instance, has a full-time staff of six professionals reporting to a board member. Affiliates also will retain advertising and public relations agencies or other professional help as required. And, as mentioned earlier, they can also call on corporate staff for professional support.

The German affiliate used all these options. The staff researched and developed the program with input and guidance from New York. The copy and much of the material was prepared by the staff. The posters, of course, were from outside illustrators. Layout, artwork, and printing of brochures also were done outside. An agency handled the modest institutional ad campaign to promote attendance at the Mobil exhibits. Press contact work was done by the staff.

Reception more open outside the United States

There is general agreement among Mobil executives that public affairs are often handled more easily abroad than in the United States, although obviously the corporation cannot speak out as forcibly abroad as it can in its own country. Those executives believe that in many countries the Mobil organization can get a more receptive audience with both the governments and citizens of other countries than it gets in the United States. In France, for example, considered by many to be somewhat anti-United States, there are civil servants who understand the oil companies better than their U.S. counterparts and consequently understand the Mobil companies there. This creates a basis for reasonable settlement of disputes that might arise.

Oil companies also get a good reception in the United Kingdom, according to a recent Mobil study. The involvement of large oil companies in the development of the North Sea oil reserves has helped that troubled economy, and the citizenry recognizes this. All European countries, Mobil reports, have shown a better-informed, less-political attitude toward the energy and oil crisis than has the United States.

With these conditions, Mobil's foreign public affairs programs have a somewhat different thrust. In the United States, the attempt is to create a basic understanding of Mobil's business. Abroad, some of this is needed, but usually more emphasis is put on attempts to set affiliates apart from other companies in a positive way. Programs frequently promote out-of-the-ordinary events that distinguish Mobil companies from others and promote their image as companies concerned with social issues. Projects that identify the local Mobil company with the aspirations of the host country are especially emphasized.

Activities frequently utilize the arts of the host country. Recently, for example, a Mobil company helped organize an Arab art exhibit in the United States. Other programs have featured the art of Indonesia, Ghana, Portugal, and Germany.

In Turkey, a Mobil company builds schools. In Japan, the Mobil affiliates sponsor student–business seminars.

Much time and effort goes into identifying the needs and interests of the host country's citizens and developing programs to meet them. When the programs are well received, they are cultivated and developed until their purpose is met. Many programs continue for years.

Part Five

How manufacturing and operations affect public affairs

A company's manufacturing and operational practices affect the public affairs function in various ways. Often, for example, manufacturing entails environmental impact. Typical of most European multinational corporations, the Swiss company, Ciba-Geigy, places responsibility for such problems at the operating unit level. The in-depth look at the company's U.S. subsidiary provided in this case shows how such a policy works at the operating level.

At Singer, the basic operating plan, which was developed in the company's earliest years and practiced for nearly a century in some countries, has proved to have significant benefits for meeting current public affairs needs. Singer is an excellent example of a successful marriage of sound business planning and sound public affairs practice.

At Pepsico, the basic operating structure is almost unique. Franchised independent businesses handle manufacturing as well as quality control and distribution. The effect is to magnify the internal jurisdictional problems found in any decentralized international operation. The effect of these problems on public affairs practices and some of the possible solutions to them are evident in the Pepsico case.

11

Singer

"Most people think of us as a local company."

World sales:	$2.5 billion
Percent sales abroad:	42
Number of employees:	86,000
Countries with subsidiaries:	21
Central office:	United States

Singer, world famous for its sewing machines, is one of the oldest multinational corporations. The company was organized in 1851, began selling its products overseas in 1853, and in 1867 built its first overseas manufacturing facility.

Singer has a history of effective public affairs practices. The company has rarely been singled out for criticism by the government or the public in countries in which it operates. It has rebounded from the ravages of two world wars, and today the company appears to be well situated to deal with the rising trend of nationalism around the world.

The groundwork for the company's record in public affairs appears to have been laid in its marketing strategy. In the 1860s, Singer began establishing its own representatives in key trading centers around the world rather than exporting to independent jobbers. From this point, expansion of overseas facilities went in two directions—to local production facilities and to local, company-owned retail outlets.

Today, Singer sewing machines are manufactured in thirteen major factories and nine major assembly plants in twenty-one countries. In addition, the company operates 3,400 retail outlets in which its products are sold. Only 1,000 of these are located in the United States. About 1,500 are in Europe and the remaining 900 are situated throughout the rest of the world. Companies in each country operate as profit centers, and management is judged on its balance sheet.

This worldwide manufacturing, distribution, and retail sales network is built almost entirely with nationals as employees. Singer is more than a household word in the United Kingdom, Germany, France, and Italy. The people who make Singer products and sell them are also the citizens of these countries. And this is the pattern all over the world—not just clerks and assembly line workers—but the very top of the organization in the country. Singer's policy is summed up by a top executive: "All things being equal, Singer would prefer in any country to have a top executive who is a national of that country."

Marketing plan aids public affairs

Singer's organization was designed as the keystone in its worldwide marketing plan. This plan, which proved successful at the outset, has been patiently implemented for more than a century. It has made the company preeminent in sewing machines. But there is an important additional benefit that may or may not have been planned that way from the outset. This network, staffed by nationals, gives the company great strength in the arena of international public affairs. In all its overseas operations, Singer acts and is treated more like a national company than a foreign company.

Currently, the toughest public affairs problem the company faces is closing several unprofitable non-sewing-machine facilities it has acquired. In these instances, the basic strength from which the company has to work becomes apparent.

In 1975, Singer decided to close a washing machine and refrigerator manufacturing plant in Leini, Italy. The closing would put 2,000 workers out of jobs. And the timing could not have been worse. Other companies were closing plants in Italy and the government was alarmed.

A committee of top executives from the United States and Italy, under the control of the European Division president, worked out the step-by-step plan of action. A policy of frankness was followed for all public and private discussions.

The Italian management director and an American executive first announced the company's decision privately to key government officials. Subsequently, all governmental agencies expected to take an interest in the matter were informed. At each level of the bureaucracy where contact was made, the company's position was carefully explained, and protocol and arrangements were agreed upon for proceeding.

Another official of the plant, an Italian national with considerable status and credibility, acted as spokeperson for all public announcements. He, of course, worked continuously with the managing director so the public statements always conformed to agreements reached with the government.

The result was government acceptance of the decision, an equitable settlement with labor, and much less publicity than accorded the closings of several plants by other multinationals at about the same time.

Public affairs aids marketing effort

In another instance, Singer closed a business machines plant in Holland. Some accompanying publicity gave the impression that Singer was going out of business entirely in Holland. Sales in Singer retail outlets there fell sharply. The company responded quickly, pointing out that it was merely closing down an unprofitable operation so that it could continue operating its other Dutch manufacturing and retail outlets. A list of Singer retail outlets was given broad distribution to show the extent of the company's commitment in the country. Benefiting from this additonal publicity, retail sales rebounded and even increased.

The problem of nationalism is one of the most important public affairs issues confronting multinationals today. Singer officials believe the problem is not as serious for Singer as it might be. In most countries where nationalism is an issue, Singer has a long-term relationship, frequently extending over a hundred years. Most people in these countries think of Singer as a local company. The company has been there "forever," and most, if not all its employees, are friends and neighbors.

Another point Singer views as a strength in this situation is that its main products, sewing machines, are generally sold to consumers rather than to the government. In many areas, this keeps Singer out of national controversies that frequently accompany large sales to foreign governments. And, finally, Singer production does not involve significant use or removal of natural resources from the country.

Reliance on local input

Singer's procedure with international public affairs problems is centralized coordination with heavy reliance on local, on-the-spot management. Local managers are expected to identify and report problems to headquarters. In most cases, they will also implement the plan of action agreed to. In particularly sensitive situations, as in Leini, Italy, an executive from regional headquarters or from the United States will be dispatched to the scene to help.

Each company manager in Singer's worldwide network is responsible for public affairs problems in his or her area. This responsibility includes identifying the problem, alerting headquarters, developing recommendations on action, and then carrying out the agreed-upon plan. In large subsidiaries, a staff assignment for public affairs is sometimes made, but it is strictly one of implementation rather than planning.

Recommendations from subsidiaries do not go directly to New York headquarters unless they are of critical importance. They are usually forwarded through regional headquarters. The largest regional headquarters is in London. That office has responsibility for all of Europe. Under most conditions, decisions on public affairs questions will be made in London and referred to New York for final approval.

Communications policy

The company has a clear policy on the release of information to the public. On matters with international implications, no statements or actions are to be made locally without first coordinating such moves through corporate headquarters. If the matter is purely local, the managing director of the local company is expected to proceed as he or she sees fit.

The company has found that the nationals who are executives in its foreign operations are extremely effective at identifying problems, accurately assesing their implications, and developing workable solutions to them. The knowledge and sensitivity of a national regarding the workings of his or her own government provide the best information on which to proceed. The company rarely uses outsiders—the United States or foreign embassies, the United Nations, or outside public relations counsel. Bankers sometimes prove to be invaluable sources of information, and the company also retains outside lawyers on occasion. But even in the Leini, Italy, closing, Singer's own labor lawyers did most of the work.

When it is necessary to communicate information to the public at large, heavy reliance is placed on the press. Releases for worldwide distribution are written in English and transmitted over the Universal News Service, with necessary and appropriate translations. Local managers are not involved in this distribution of news.

In Singer's international public affairs practices, two basic strengths stand out: The company's heavy employment of nationals and the familiarity of the public with the company through its major product line. The public affairs function is geared to capitalizing fully on these strengths.

12

Ciba-Geigy

"When in Rome . . ."

> World sales: $5.3 billion
> Percent sales abroad: 98
> Number of employees: 75,000
> Countries with subsidiaries: Over 100
> Central office: Switzerland

The Ciba-Geigy Group has annual sales of about $5.3 billion. About 98 percent of sales occur outside Switzerland, the company's home country. Of its 75,000 employees, fewer than one-third, about 22,000 work in Switzerland. The company's major product lines, in descending order of sales volume, are: pharmaceuticals, agricultural chemicals, dyestuffs and chemicals, plastics and additives, photographic products, and Airwick consumer products. The product groups with the highest rate of growth at present are plastics and additives, pharmaceuticals, and consumer products.

By any measure Ciba-Geigy is a major multinational corporation, and it is heavily engaged in two of the world's most sensitive product areas—health and food. Product safety, consumer protection, and environmental protection are vital issues.

Public affairs, therefore, is an important function at Ciba-Geigy. Typical of European multinationals, Ciba-Geigy integrates much of the function into line management responsibility rather than staff. While there is an information and promotion department at group headquarters in Basel, the executive committee of the company identifies priorities, sets policy, and determines actions. The information and promotion department gathers information for the committee and implements action as directed.

The company is organized geographically into six major regions. Countries within a region and even major divisions and plant sites within the countries have people on staff who carry out public affairs activities. They are responsible to and report to the unit manager at their location.

The company is also organized by business lines with an operating committee for each major division. This structure also is repeated in regions and countries throughout the world network. Divisions are responsible for public affairs matters relating to their products. And they have public affairs specialists on staff to deal with those matters.

Major problems concerning worldwide markets or operations are handled at the highest corporate level. Regional and national matters, however, are dealt with at the regional or national level affected by the situation.

Assignment of responsibility

The positioning of public affairs staff in the organization follows the assignment of responsibility. The reasoning is that some problems are product related and, therefore, are the responsibility of division-management. Others are social or political and not related to a specific product. The latter are the responsibility of regional or national management.

In practice, however, many situations require shared interests and responsibilities. If a major problem occurs with a specific product in a country, that country's manager, as well as the division manager, is quite naturally concerned. It is a very short distance from attitudes that question one product to attitudes that question other company products.

As a consequence, coordination between division, national, and regional management is common. In the process, there is considerable use of public affairs staff. The public affairs function becomes a central point for gathering information inside and outside the company and for coordinating planning, as well as carrying out the action, once a course is determined.

How the organization works

The company's approach to environmental protection shows how this process works. The issue is one of continuing concern. Environmental problems cross jurisdictional lines. They can originate at a plant, which would be a regional responsibility, or with a product, such as an insecticide, which would be a division's responsibility. All of this must be coordinated at the corporate level.

In the view of the corporation, solving an environmental problem is essentially a technical matter. A staff group of technical experts has been set up at Basel to deal specifically with the various environmental needs and the problems the company encounters around the world. The staff expertise spans both product and operating technology. As the group develops the technology to deal with a problem, the information is referred to the executive committee, and the executive committee directs dissemination of the information. It is made available to plant and division personnel throughout the organization who have an interest in the problem and, if the executive committee so directs, the information is made public.

In such cases, the technology is not only developed at corporate headquarters, but policy on internal and external uses of the technology is set there as well. Once this is established, people with regional, divisional, or public affairs responsibilities follow the policy.

How a major subsidiary operates

How does this plan work in the field, that is, within a major subsidiary? A detailed examination of Ciba-Geigy's largest subsidiary, Ciba-Geigy Corporation in the United States, provides a good illustration.

The U.S. subsidiary is a sizable chemical company in its own right. It employs some 10,000 people, and sales approach the billion dollar mark.

The company is organized by operating divisions along the same lines as the parent with the exception of the photographic group, which reports to its parent in the United Kingdom rather than to the U.S. corporation.

U.S. sales also reflect a different order of importance than that found in the parent company. Agricultural chemicals are the sales leader in the United States followed by pharmaceuticals, dyestuffs and chemicals, plastics and additives, and Airwick consumer products.

The organization and operation of the various aspects of public affairs also reflect the approach established by the parent company. Responsibilities are variously assigned to the corporate staff, the division level, and the plant level. Assignments of responsibility for a subject area or issue generally reflect the evolutionary importance and social impact of the issue.

The most firmly established public affairs activities are those dealing with regulatory requirements in effect for some time, i.e., those involving pharmaceuticals and agricultural chemicals. In pharmaceuticals, where public as well as governmental concern has a longer history, Ciba-Geigy has a vice-president of public affairs with a director of public relations and a director of governmental relations reporting to the vice-president. In agricultural chemicals where public concern has a shorter history, public relations reports to marketing, while government relations comes under product research and development.

Functions grow from needs

It is not difficult to trace the development and assignment of these responsibilities. The primary original reason for a public relations function in a product group was support of the marketing effort. So this responsibility was assigned to the marketing department. The government relations function was primarily a job of shepherding a new product through the intricacies of testing and winning governmental sanction. Product research and development was the logical place to assign this function.

That structure still exists in agricultural chemicals. In pharmaceuticals, circumstances have led to further developments, and the functions have become more highly centralized and specialized to deal with the broader concerns encountered today.

With the proliferation of regulations that cover broader issues rather than a particular product and with the rise of the concept of a manufacturer's liability for problems resulting from the use of its products, another level of review has been instituted. Responsibility for this level is assigned to corporate counsel. While the division and site managers remain responsible for the specific impact of their product or plant, corporate counsel is responsible for reviewing the implications of new regulations, their interrelationships within the broad context of evolving law, and court decisions. Corporate counsel is vested with a power to approve initiatives proposed by plant and product managers.

As the broad social movements of the last decade have become formalized in new laws relating to the manufacture and use of chemicals and toxic substances, Ciba-Geigy found it advisable to organize a new staff department to deal specifically with these matters. It is called the safety, health, and ecology department. This department has its own government relations function concerned with federal legislation. Its actions and initiatives are also subject to review and approval by corporate counsel.

Other interests of the U.S. company in the area of public affairs are the responsibility of the corporate relations department, which is the U.S. counterpart of the information and promotion department in Basel. This department is concerned with the increasing importance of public opinion and its impact on the business environment. Today, the public has a strong influence on where a plant can be built, on what changes or additions can be made in an existing plant, and even on what products can be manufactured there. Dealing with these matters calls for expertise in public communications. As a result, the public information function in the corporate relations department is playing an increasingly important role.

Committee coordinates resources

All these organizational changes and developments show how the crosscurrents of social demand have brought more of the functions of the company into play to secure a continuing franchise for operating the business. In an attempt to coordinate all these resources, Ciba-Geigy has organized a corporate public affairs committee. The committee is composed of the vice-president for administration, the vice-presidents of the two major divisions, the corporate vice-president and counsel, the director of corporate relations, and the public affairs manager.

The committee serves as a central point where all the various factors affecting an issue can be interrelated and evaluated for determining a course of action. The committee has no jurisdiction over operating units, and, as a committee, cannot call for action to be taken by various units of the company. Some of its members, however, do have operational authority and jurisdiction. So, for example, when all factors and interrelationships affecting the production or sale of an agricultural chemical are evaluated by the committee and a course of action agreed upon, the agricultural division vice-president, who is a member of the committee, can see to it that the recommendations are followed at the operating level.

While the corporate relations people exercise no direct control through the committee, they do influence committee decisions and recommendations.

In matters relating to state, federal, and local laws and regulations, the U.S. subsidiary acts autonomously. Activities in these areas are not strongly influenced by the parent company. Though corporate and divison personnel coordinate and interrelate frequently and closely with their counterparts in Basel on other matters because of their unique nature, decisions concerning U.S. law and regulations are made and implemented on the national level.

Role of corporate relations

The corporate relations department handles communications of a companywide or corporate nature but does not participate in individual division activities or site-directed efforts unless asked to. As a matter of practice, division and site executives do request and get help regularly from the corporate relations department, but they are not required to seek advice nor are they required to follow the advice given.

The corporate relations department services the press on corporate matters, produces internal and external corporate communications, and handles community relations for the corporate headquarters site and public affairs matters of a corporate nature. Because the company is a wholly owned subsidiary of the Swiss parent, no major program is directed to the U.S. investment community.

Operating units inform the press on matters relating to their products or plants and handle local community relations. The corporate relations department advises and assists as requested and serves as an example and resource for planning and implementation.

Company political action program

Political action gives an example of how this works. A worldwide corporate policy of Ciba-Geigy is to encourage employees to take part in political and governmental affairs and in civic and community activities. This activity is entirely on a voluntary basis, and employees are completely free to select the party, candidate, or issue in which they are interested. In the American subsidiary, an action program has been instituted to implement this policy. Communications to employees at all locations in the United States attempt to inform them on election issues and give them background about the candidates running for office. Employees are urged to make their views known to public officials, to register and vote in elections, and to contribute time and money to the candidates of their choice.

At headquarters, the corporate relations department develops information on candidates and election issues for dissemination to employees and arranges voter registration drives, candidate appearances, and other activities. The department also administers the Employee Good Government Fund through which employees can make political contributions.

The department also encourages and assists executives at other locations in setting up and conducting similar programs. As in all public affairs activities, the decision on whether to conduct such a campaign and the scope it is to take remains with the operating unit manager.

Influence of size and ownership

Two influences are strikingly apparent in this example of a subsidiary operation, and both are probably pertinent to most offshore operations of a major multinational corporation.

First is the relative size of the company. While the U.S. company is Ciba-Geigy's largest subsidiary, it is not large in comparison with other U.S. chemical companies. Though in some product areas size is a major factor, it is not a dominant one.

As such, the company simply is not in a position to exert public affairs leadership. Ciba-Geigy certainly has its own very solid position, which it acts to protect, but it would be outgunned if it attempted to go beyond that and lead or influence the general trend of events. For this reason it is important for the company to be active in trade groups and trade associations.

The second influence is that of the parent company. While the American company is fairly autonomous, the hand of the parent is there. The American company does not respond to American stockholders. Rather, it responds to the parent company, which is the sole stockholder. The expectations of the parent company would appear to be conservative; the basic requirement, return on investment. Ciba-Geigy has not come to the United States to espouse a new way of doing business or to advance a pet belief. It has come to the United States to sell its products. The company is a guest and will observe the customs and practices of the host country. In keeping with policy, Ciba-Geigy has developed the appropriate and necessary response mechanisms.

Keeping in touch

This posture is typical of multinational corporations in regard to their offshore subsidiaries. Managers are constantly reminded that, "We are guests in the host country." The implications of that position are reinforced by the fact that the subsidiary so often is a small operation in relation to its competitors in the host country. The result is a public affairs program more aptly described as compliant rather than vigorous.

While the evolution of response mechanisms in Ciba-Geigy's American subsidiary directly relates to its external needs, one must ask if the resulting accumulation of internal procedures is the most efficient and effective use of the company's resources. There is a growing feeling that the U.S. government should stand back, look at itself and the proliferating, often contradictory, requirements it makes of businesses and somehow streamline the process. A company that builds its public affairs program on the basis of responding to such varying requirements could profit from some serious rethinking and reorganization on the part of the government.

13

PepsiCo, Inc.

"Franchising multiplies problems."

World sales: $4.3 billion
Percent sales abroad: 25
Number of employees: 92,000
Countries with subsidiaries: 19
Central office: United States

The taproot of PepsiCo, Inc., is the soft drink, Pepsi-Cola. Working from this base, the company has diversified broadly in recent years. Today, there are five major product divisions. The beverages group is still the largest, accounting for nearly half the company's revenues. In addition to Pepsi-Cola, however, other soft drinks are being produced. The other four product divisions are snack foods (Frito-Lay), sporting goods (Wilson), trucking (North American Van Lines and Lee Way Motor Freight) and pizza restaurants (Pizza Hut).

The last, Pizza Hut, is a recent acquisition. It is the largest pizza restaurant chain in the world, with major operations in the United States and Canada and developmental operations in other parts of the world.

It was necessary for PepsiCo, Inc. to divest itself of its alcoholic beverages division in the United States in the course of acquiring Pizza Hut. A number of state regulations prohibit wholesale and retail food and liquor operations under the same ownership. PepsiCo was nevertheless able to continue its alcoholic beverages operations outside the United States. Under the present organization, the company continues to import Russian vodka and most of the products that are distributed in the United States by Monsieur Henri, Ltd.

In the United States, PepsiCo's operating divisions are autonomous and decentralized. Outside the United States, these operations are consolidated under the international division headed by a corporate vice-president. Foreign operations account for nearly 25 percent of corporate sales and, here again, beverages are the largest segment, producing overseas sales approaching domestic volume.

The organization of the company's soft drink operation is quite different from that of most other companies. PepsiCo does not distribute or retail its soft drink directly to consumers. Instead, it grants territorial franchises to independent business operations and supplies them with the concentrate to make beverages. These bottlers mix, package, and distribute the product in their market areas. Marketing responsibilities are shared. PepsiCo produces and runs national advertising, while the bottlers are responsible for field salespersons, local advertising, and promotional activities.

This system results in a distinctive organization. PepsiCo depends largely on its good name (its franchise with the public) for business. The company has an enormous investment in this. Yet, two key elements in upholding this franchise are virtually out of PepsiCo's hands. The final manufacture of the product and its distribution to the consumer are in the hands of independent businesses over which PepsiCo has no operational control.

This distinction may seem more apparent than real. The good name of PepsiCo products is as important to the bottler as it is to PepsiCo. If PepsiCo were discredited with the public, for example, the franchise would have little or no value. Therefore, it behooves both parties to work toward and support good public affairs practices. One of the first considerations in this regard is strict quality procedures which PepsiCo has established and maintains among its bottlers worldwide.

Beyond this basic principle of providing a high-quality product, agreement on what constitutes "good" or "necessary" public affairs practice does not always occur.

Today in the United States there would be general agreement that high standards of quality control in a food product must be observed at all times. This is accepted as an essential part of doing business. But when a more complex issue such as the environmental impact of nonreturnable containers is raised, a consensus among the corporation and independent bottlers might not be so readily achieved. Over 400 independent bottlers operate in the United States, each with its own distinctive capabilities and resources and each concerned primarily with the issues it faces in its market area.

The company's soft drink operations outside the United States are even more complex. More than 500 bottling operations exist in 136 countries and territories. These franchise holders span virtually every conceivable cultural, ethnic, and political persuasion. This dictates a two-tier approach to public affairs: first, an individual, country-by-country program dealing with national problems and closely coordinated with the bottler; and an international program, designed and implemented by PepsiCo alone.

Another factor is inherent in the company's manufacturing and operating procedures which affect the over-all public affairs situation faced by PepsiCo. In international operations, this is a plus factor. The franchise approach provides a strong basis for dealing with the issue of nationalism. Franchised bottlers are nationals who own and operate their own businesses. They are not employees of a foreign-owned corporation. PepsiCo provides the raw materials (concentrate) and manufacturing know-how (sound, sanitary product practices), and marketing assistance and guidance. By providing these, PepsiCo helps create local business and employment. In other words, the company enjoys a position that preempts many of the issues faced by multinationals around the world. In this situation, about the only area in which contention might occur is in how much PepsiCo would be permitted to charge local bottling companies for what the company provides.

The franchise approach in international expansion is equally adaptable to socialist countries where there is no private ownership. In some countries, arrangements are made directly with the government. The state rather than a private organization becomes the franchised bottler.

The public affairs function does not play a major role in operations in socialist countries. Top PepsiCo management is personally involved in these negotiations.

It is a long process, beginning sometimes with the head of state, certainly with a cabinet minister, and gradually working down into the bureaucracy where actions are implemented. In the initial stages of such negotiations, the chief executive participates. After the basic arrangements are agreed upon, International Division management takes over and sees the project through. The contractual arrangements in socialist countries are identical to those made by PepsiCo with independent businesspersons in other parts of the world. Sometimes, however, it is necessary to make barter arrangements rather than cash payments because the particular country lacks foreign exchange.

Product affects public affairs situation

The over-all public affairs situation faced by the beverages group is also influenced by the product itself. Consumers don't need soft drinks in the sense they need an automobile and gasoline if they are to get back and forth to work. Soft drinks are pleasant and relaxing and fun but they rarely qualify as essential. These drinks, therefore, are especially vulnerable to attack in the public arena. It is extremely difficult to muster a constituency of support for "fun and relaxation" if it is allegedly interfering with some "greater purpose" such as cleaning up the environment or ensuring healthy diets for children.

Issues like these are of much greater concern in the United States and other developed countries, and PepsiCo has an extensive organization to deal with these matters where they arise.

However, the soft drink products of PepsiCo at times represent a plus factor for consumers in foreign countries. Sanitarily prepared and packaged soft drinks frequently offer an alternative to bad drinking water or excessive consumption of alcoholic beverages. In countries where one or both of these problems exist, soft drinks become more than just fun and relaxation. Introducing soft drinks to the population can represent an improvement the government views as significant and important. Conditions such as these help to win government endorsement and support.

The basic thrust of public affairs function is country-by-country support of PepsiCo's international operations. The public affairs effort is concentrated on the problems and opportunities that arise in each country where PepsiCo does business.

The PepsiCo public affairs organization is structured so that country-by-country problems are dealt with as much as possible at the national level. The corporate public affairs function is a resource that can be drawn upon when it is needed in a specific instance. Otherwise, the corporate public affairs department does not become actively involved when the issue is localized in a single country. When the issue transcends national boundaries and involves PepsiCo as the multinational entity, the corporate public affairs department becomes actively involved.

The Arab boycott provides an example of such an occasion. Some Arab states imposed a boycott on doing business with companies that also traded with Israel. American multinational corporations were forbidden by the United States government to observe this boycott. PepsiCo has some bottlers in Arab countries but none in Israel. The company was questioned on its actions.

PepsiCo's position was a result of business decisions. The company's marketing studies had shown Israel to be a small market already well served by local and other international suppliers. A number of Arab countries, on the other hand, were relatively open. PepsiCo went where the markets for bottling operations were more promising. So far as Israel was concerned, PepsiCo took another approach. The company developed substantial trade with Israel in essential vegetable oils and other raw materials needed by Israeli soft drink producers.

Explaining the company position and all its ramifications became the job of the corporate public affairs department.

PepsiCo sees a growing worldwide trend in government regulation of products such as those it sells. The greatest activity in this regard is presently in the United States and Canada. Japan and a number of European countries are paying more and more attention to questions relating to food ingredients and environmental impact. And the World Health Organization is setting standards for ingredients in food products on a worldwide scale.

The experience PepsiCo gains in dealing with these issues in the United States is transferable to other countries where they arise. The issue of disposable containers provides an example. Canada and the United Kingdom currently are becoming more concerned about this problem. Policies, programs, background information, and even creative material developed in connection with the issue in the United States are being made available for use in both those countries.

Public affairs issues will probably arise more frequently overseas as PepsiCo's operations grow and expand. As this happens, it is likely that involvement on the part of corporate headquarters will become more common. In any event, the task of enlisting bottlers in the cause and making active and effective allies of them will continue to be the first order of business. This policy may be more akin to diplomacy than to public affairs, but it must come first if the company's communications efforts are to be effective.

Part Six

How the presence of a company affects
its public affairs

The impact on the public affairs function of the characteristic we call "presence" is illustrated in these last three cases.

Dow Corning is a company new to the international scene with a low degree of presence. Deere is entering the intermediate stage, rapidly expanding its operations. In its use of outside public affairs counsel, it has perhaps discovered a shortcut to identifying and dealing effectively with the many problems posed by rapid expansion. At BASF, we see the stage of presence we call "maturity." This stage follows a period of rapid and extensive worldwide expansion. The emphasis in public affairs switches from growth to consolidation.

14

Dow Corning

"Total communications"

World sales: $479 million
Percent sales abroad: 40
Number of employees: 4,000
Countries with subsidiaries: 13
Central office: United States

Dow Corning is a young company in an industry no older than itself. The company's business is built on an unusual family of chemical polymers, called silicones, which it developed and introduced as a commercial product in 1943.

The company itself is a joint venture of two major American corporations. Though modest in comparison with other multinational corporations examined in this study, it nevertheless is a sizable business in its own right. Dow Corning operates in 21 countries (subsidiaries in 13) and employs more than 4,000 people. Although international operations received no major emphasis until the 1960s, about 40 percent of revenues are now generated abroad.

Silicones, the chemical family upon which the business is built, have a broad range of application, and Dow Corning introduces new products to the world at a rapid rate. In its early history the company grew as fast as new applications could be identified and made commercially feasible. Today, more research, development, and marketing effort is required to identify opportunities and take advantage of them. As a consequence, growth is somewhat slower, though still very good by almost any business standard.

Dow Corning has embarked on an adventure. The company's challenge is to identify potential applications for a family of chemicals it discovered and then develop products to meet the need. Both are highly technical tasks. To succeed, the company must be creative, resourceful, and prudent. It has been staffed accordingly. More than 25 percent of the personnel have at least one college degree; more than 10 percent have advanced degrees. The challenge now is to make the most of the company's resources and opportunities.

What is the role of public affairs in such a situation? As noted in other operations, the needs of the company dictate the scope and nature of the function. Dow Corning operates under the management philosophy of hiring good people, then giving them the latitude and freedom to exercise their talents. Decisions are made as close to the point of the action as possible. Usually, these decisions are based on a consensus of middle management.

This philosophy is applied to the total operation, including the public affairs activity. In short, public affairs decisions are made by the people involved in and confronted by the issue.

Dow Corning believes this operational philosophy calls for total communication effort: the development of guidelines or a code in relation to which decisions can be made; an extensive internal communications program to ensure that the people who make decisions have all the information they need to make the correct decision; and an effort to ensure that the public is made aware of Dow Corning programs and achievements.

This "total" communications concept of Dow Corning is not a one-way flow of information. Efforts in all three areas begin with listening to the target audience, and such efforts are carefully designed to be responsive to the expectations of the audiences to whom they are addressed.

Developing a code

The procedures followed by the company in developing a code of conduct illustrate how Dow Corning goes about being responsive to the audience. A task force was appointed by the chief executive officer to supervise the development of a code of conduct for the company. The task force made a detailed review of codes and guidelines developed by other companies—Caterpillar, for example—and by organizations such as The International Chamber of Commerce and OECD.

Drawing on the information obtained from these reviews and on discussions that identified needs peculiar to Dow Corning, management drafted a letter outlining what a company code should cover and what it should attempt to accomplish. The letter was sent by the chief executive to all company managers around the world with a request that they respond with their views on what should be set forth in the Dow Corning code.

Response to the letter gave the task force the information it believed was essential to develop a sound, workable code for the company. As the code takes shape from this input, guidelines are emerging on two levels. The first level cites basic principles of business operation that all Dow Corning employees around the world are expected to follow. The second level consists of regional guidelines, specific principles that respond to the cultural characteristics of a region of the world. These, in addition to the general principles, are to be observed by employees in the region to which the specific guidelines pertain.

Internal communications

Another example of the company's determination to be responsive to its audience is evident in Dow Corning's internal communications. Face-to-face exchanges are encouraged at all levels, and the company regularly uses opinion surveys to make formal, objective measurements of employee attitudes. Recently, Dow Corning completed two studies of its employees. One probed how employees felt Dow Corning should be functioning as a business and as an employer. The other study measured employee attitudes about how the company goes about meeting its social responsibilities.

Results of these studies are taken into account in management decisions regarding the direction of the company. They also provide essential information for developing communications programs for employees.

Dow Corning uses employee newspapers, video tapes and cable TV, fact sheets and bulletins to keep employees abreast of developments within the company. The communications cover worldwide company operations, and the communications are disseminated to employees on a worldwide basis.

A special feature of the employee newspaper invites employees to submit questions to management and guarantees management answers without disclosing the identity of the questioner. Information booklets and brochures are provided on specific topics of particular interest. Benefit program information is sent to the employee's home so the person's spouse will also be kept up-to-date on current benefits.

Dow Corning encourages its managers to hold frequent meetings with employees. It provides training to equip managers better to hold such meetings and to encourage a two-way flow of information. The company also schedules five to six instructive presentations each year by management for salaried employees. For some meetings, spouses are also invited. The presentations review accomplishment and past performance and outline the plans and outlook for the future. The sessions also serve as opportunities for employees to voice their ideas, opinions, and reactions to the reports. The meetings are videotaped and tapes are distributed worldwide.

To provide background and depth for decision making, a series of educational programs is provided for employees. In addition to covering the usual managerial skills, the programs also include such topics as economics and political science.

Recently the government relations department trained two dozen employees to act as conference leaders in a specially prepared political affairs program. Periodically that department also presents (via the video network) information about the actions in Washington, D.C., or state capitals that may affect the business, the employee, or both. With a better understanding of what is taking place in government, Dow Corning executives believe that they as well as their employees will act and react when appropriate.

The general practice of open and candid communications throughout the company is regarded by management as a key element in the company's success.

External communications

Because Dow Corning is a highly technical company and most of its products are used industrially, it has a low public identity. The company maintains a vigorous effort, however, to supply technical information about its products to the trade press. Also, a company magazine, *Material News,* is published every two months for an audience of 60,000 around the world.

In areas where public interest can be anticipated, Dow Corning develops special programs. For example, when potential medical uses of silicones were first investigated, Dow Corning recognized that interest on the part of a new audience—the medical profession—would be high. The company set up a department to help physicians become familiar with this work. Called the Center for Aid to Medical Research, this effort antedated Dow Corning's commercial entry into the medical field by several years.

A silicone display at the Chicago Museum of Science and Industry and another at the Corning Glass Museum in Corning, New York, are maintained for general public interest. A speakers bureau offers company talent at no cost to the community. The company's college relations program presents grants-in-aid to departments of various colleges. These grants are generally unrestricted but have resulted in recruiting a number of technical employees for the company.

A foundation for the future

The core of the Dow Corning communications effort is developed at corporate headquarters. From there the operation gradually moves to other locations around the world. People assigned to the public affairs staff at locations outside the United States report to the regional manager and only indirectly to corporate headquarters, but the principles, operating procedures, and much of the material developed at headquarters are used worldwide.

Dow Corning faces little in the way of major ongoing public affairs problems, partly because of the nature of the industry and the product line, but also because the company strives to maintain high operating, health, and product standards. Because the same standards in such areas as pollution control, product quality, and employee concern are practiced on a worldwide basis, the company believes it has established excellent relationships in all countries and communities in which it is located.

At this stage in the company's development, public affairs management believes it should concentrate on such things as a code of conduct, responsible advertising and sales practices, and employee and community education. The objective is to prevent problems that could arise in the future, so far as this is possible, and at the same time build a sound basis for dealing with those problems that cannot be anticipated.

15

Deere & Company

"Decisions at the point of action"

World sales: $4.2 billion
Percent sales abroad: 30
Number of employees: 59,000
Countries with subsidiaries: 16
Central office: United States

Overseas sales at Deere & Company are about 30 percent of total volume, and international business has been growing rapidly. In 1978, overseas sales of $1.26 billion (out of $4.2 billion for the total company) were 390 percent greater than in 1972 ($257 million).

Deere is the world's largest manufacturer of farm machinery. With the growing world demand for food and fiber, the outlook is bright for products that carry the name of John Deere, the blacksmith who founded the company in 1837.

The Deere company is highly integrated in the industrial sense. It manufactures most of the components for its products, including engines, transmissions, castings, and even nuts and bolts. Deere's major manufacturing facilities are in the United States and Canada but the company also has manufacturing and assembly plants in nine other countries outside North America. The sales network comprises some 5,000 independent dealers in more than 100 countries who are supported by sales branches in 25 countries.

For administrative purposes, Deere has separated the foreign operations of its agricultural and consumer products divisions into two regions. Region I covers Latin America, Australia, and the Far East. The managing director of that region operates from company headquarters in Moline, Illinois. Region II covers Europe, Africa, and the Middle East, and its managing director is headquartered in Mannheim, Germany. The industrial equipment division maintains its headquarters in Brussels. That office was established to increase emphasis on the development of markets for construction, forestry, and utility equipment in Europe, Africa, and the Middle East.

107

Decentralization applies to public affairs

Deere is a decentralized operation. Each operating unit—manufacturing plant, distribution center, sales office, and so on—has profit responsibility for its operations. Along with this responsibility, managers have substantial decision-making authority. It is company policy that operating decisions should be made as close to the point of action as possible and at the lowest organizational level at which the necessary information is available and can be properly evaluated.

This policy also applies to the public affairs function. The front-line organizational force is the manager in each country where the company has operations. This is the point "closest to the action." Rather than developing a public relations staff at national levels, however, public relations agencies are retained in several countries to work with management. Activities typically undertaken in a country encompass such programs as product publicity, employee communications, governmental relations, and public affairs.

Administratively, public relations activities are supervised by a regional public relations director. In Region II, this person, headquartered in Mannheim, reports to the regional managing director there and also reports on a dotted-line basis to the director of public relations overseas at corporate headquarters in Moline. Neither of these administrators has a staff for implementing public relations activities. They advise and counsel and rely entirely on country-level staff and public relations agencies for the implementation of activities.

Extensive use of national agencies

Of the companies covered in this study, Deere makes the most extensive use of public relations agencies in host countries. As its international operations have expanded, the company has found marked differences in operating environments from one country to another. Each country has distinct and characteristic needs in product publicity, governmental requirements, and labor relations.

As Deere puts it, "We don't need standardized international thinking in public affairs. We need specific country and area thinking."

The most cost-effective means of obtaining the level of expertise Deere needs in a given country, the company has found, is to retain a local public relations agency. Local agencies, Deere reports, understand national media, the role of government, and labor needs and they have good contacts in all these areas.

Deere insists on dealing with the top person in each agency it retains and works toward a long-term relationship. Deere goes to great lengths to indoctrinate its agencies' personnel in the company's products and operating procedures. The company's public relations director for overseas operations spends considerable time with them, and frequently all agency representatives are flown to Moline for an indoctrination and planning session. On an operating basis, however, work is mostly planned and implemented at the country level with the local Deere management.

The organization in action

An example shows how this approach works. In 1975, a downturn in the economy made it necessary for Deere to lay off 68 people in its plant near Chartres, France. In France, a company must have governmental approval to discharge employees. The situation was complicated by the fact that President Giscard d'Estaing had recently declared that there was no unemployment in France.

The managing director of France reviewed the situation with his agency and staff. The plant could not continue to operate without this temporary cutback. A decision was made to spell out clearly to the proper officials the economic facts of the matter.

At meetings with unions and government officials, the facts were presented. An arrangement was reached that allowed the cutback. There was no publicity on the layoff from the company, the union, or the government. As soon as business conditions permitted, the employees were called back.

This is the company approach to solving problems as it is intended to work: analysis of the problem and development of a plan of action are completed at the point where the problem arises. When there are possible serious consequences, as in the Chartres instance, regional headquarters is advised. Once the plan is agreed to, it is implemented on the scene.

In this case, the measure of success was the minimum amount of disruption to the company, the community, and the government and union officials involved.

Policy guides prepared by headquarters

The decisions managers make in such matters are expected to comply with company policy. To ensure that managers are completely familiar with these policies, a series of bulletins has been issued. Taken together these bulletins constitute a sort of policy book for Deere's worldwide operations.

Deere entered the international business at a much later date than its major competitors. Since the company undertook concerted international business development efforts 21 years ago, it has concentrated its efforts on becoming firmly established in overseas markets. Deere has found that, as company operations continue to grow, they have a greater impact on the political, social, and economic structures of their host countries. And public affairs activities must be expanded accordingly.

Today, the company has established a public affairs function that meets present needs and at the same time builds a foundation that will support substantially increased Deere operations in the future.

16

BASF

"Make company operations transparent."

World sales:	$11.3 billion
Number of employees:	165,000
Countries with subsidiaries:	140
Central office:	Federal Republic of Germany

BASF is one of the prime examples of "the economic miracle of Germany," and this is reflected in the company's communications efforts. BASF had long been a world leader in chemicals, but the close of World War II found the company with 94 percent of its plants destroyed or damaged by bombing. The company began a period of rebuilding. Communications efforts were directed internally, to a large extent, getting employees to pull together for the job they faced.

As the company got back on its feet, it entered a period of phenomenal growth and worldwide expansion. Communications turned to the outside—selling BASF products, technology, and efficiency and building confidence in the company among investors so that capital needs could be met. By 1975 the company was operating worldwide through more than 300 affiliates, and sales passed the $8 billion mark.

With this growth, of course, came the problems of bigness—expectations from governments and the public that sometimes overreached what the company could appropriately do.

As a consequence, the company has entered another phase, a phase it calls "transparency." Management believes it must bring outside publics inside the company and show them how it really works. The company must educate those nonmarket publics that can affect its future—government officials, public interest advocates, union leaders. These groups must understand the needs of the company as well as its contributions so that unreasonable demands do not stop or reverse the trend of progress.

Elucidating company actions

In the view of BASF management, transparency is largely a process of communicating facts about what the company has already done rather than setting out to correct problems. In other words, management does not believe it has neglected needs. It believes, rather, that what has been done to meet the needs of society is not clearly understood.

For example, environmental pollution is one of the the major issues facing chemical companies. BASF points to what it has done at Ludwigshafen, the site of the giant chemical complex that is the nerve center of the company. Twenty years ago, air pollution in Ludwigshafen was extreme. Today it has been reduced to 4 percent. A persistent remaining problem of odor constitutes no threat to human health.

The company draws huge quantities of water from the Rhine River. About 90 percent of the water restored to the river is cleaner than the water the company draws from the river, and the remaining 10 percent is treated to be compatible with the receiving waters.

To be sure, Ludwigshafen is the company's flagship operation. The facility covers 2.3 square miles and is probably the largest chemical complex in the Western world. It has 1,500 buildings, including some 300 plants plus research units and experimental facilities. Because the company's research is centered here, it would follow that its most advanced efforts in pollution control equipment and techniques would be here too. The equipment, the techniques and the standards set here are followed in the company's other operations around the world.

Management believes that the company is a leader in environmental protection, and the more people learn about this leadership, the better BASF will appear in the public eye.

Consumer protection and product and worker safety also are issues confronting chemical companies around the world. BASF believes it is well ahead in each of these areas, as well. The task the company faces, as management sees it, is identifying the target audiences and communciating its story.

Organizing communications functions

The organization to accomplish this task—and to deal with day-to-day public affairs and public relations tasks—is controlled from corporate headquarters in Ludwigshafen. The director of the department reports to the chief executive officer. The director heads a 110-person staff at corporate headquarters and has functional responsibility for more than 50 public relations executives and their staffs in affiliated companies around the world. The staff at corporate headquarters provides services to affiliates all over the world.

The film department circulates worldwide 5,500 copies of 90

BASF-produced films. The films are viewed by five million people annually in more than 100 countries.

As many as 40,000 visitors from all over the world tour the Ludwigshafen plant each year. The tours are organized and conducted by the public relations department. Staff-produced magazines and house publications have a combined print run of 160,000 copies. Some of these appear monthly; others bimonthly or quarterly. On average, the department issues 16 to 20 booklets and other publications each year in several languages; total circulation is 1.6 million.

The department also sponsors some 1,500 projects (exclusive of research grants) at schools, universities, and institutes around the world at a cost of about $1.6 million per year.

The press department maintains contact with about 800 editorial offices and newspapers at home and abroad as well as with magazines, television stations, and wire services. Each year some 2,000 journalists come to Ludwigshafen with inquiries or requests for interviews.

Centralized supervision

The headquarters staff includes a cadre of regional coordinators. Each is assigned a group of countries. The coordinators travel extensively in their areas for periodic meetings with local public relations managers. They review past activities, discuss developments, seek out opportunities, and lay plans for projects in areas where coordination with the central office will be helpful or necessary.

The executives in charge of public relations activities at affiliates report functionally to the director at corporate headquarters. The local manager has administrative responsibility for the public relations staff and is the decision maker on local policy issues. In corporate matters, policy is set at headquarters and implementation is adapted to local conditions by the local manager and the public relations executive. The latitude given local executives in making decisions varies from country to country. Generally, the larger the subsidiary, the more sophisticated and more self-reliant the public relations staff and the more autonomous the operation.

In addition to its written policy statements and the visits by regional coordinators, the company monitors worldwide public relations activities through budget control. Projected expenses for each local public relations program, broken down by job function and administrative and operating costs, are submitted annually to the central office for approval. Quarterly, the same form is filed, showing actual expenses against the budget to date.

To guide its conduct, BASF adheres to common standards of ethics. Internationally, it follows the OECD code.

Situation plus company beliefs equal policy position

Public relations problems are solved on the basis of the best available information obtainable inside or outside the company. Generally, public affairs does its own research, planning, and execution. For particular projects or problems, however, especially in countries where the affiliate staff lacks sufficient expertise, outside assistance is retained. Such instances are the exception rather than the rule.

BASF recognizes itself as a major multinational corporation. It takes this position openly and aggressively. The company believes it has nothing to hide and holds that its goal of transparency is of key importance to its future. Management feels that the better the understanding people have of the company and how it operates, the more confidence they will place in its decisions and actions. As a consequence, BASF aggressively pursues opportunities to explain itself and its operation to key publics.

In 1974 the government of Germany held hearings on the activities and influence of German multinational companies operating in developing countries. BASF volunteered to testify at those hearings. The company did so for two reasons: to participate in public discussions about multinational corporations and to make its position as a multinational company better known to this very important audience.

Testimony was prepared with information from the legal, finance, operations, and public relations departments. The finished document constituted a detailed record of BASF as a multinational corporation. It was presented at the hearings by the director for overseas operations. The testimony, plus the director's responses to questions during the hearings, received extensive favorable coverage. The testimony was subsequently published in booklet form and widely distributed by the company.

Transparency on trial

BASF is pursuing this policy of transparency around the world. Rather than attempting to anticipate, identify, and deal with specific issues, the company seems to be attempting to establish a platform of public confidence and support from which it can deal effectively with any issues that might arise.

Such an approach has two critical requisites. First, the company's house must be in order. If it isn't, transparency could prove troublesome. Second, transparency must be total. Screening out areas from public view is unlikely to go unnoticed, and the fact that some things are being withheld would tend to increase suspicion.

Some managers might hold that a company cannot meet both requisites. It would seem that transparency would inevitably cause special problems so far as competitors are concerned. BASF set out on this course only a year ago. It is too early to tell how well it can be carried out and how effective it will be in producing the envisioned results. But, one would hope that there is a place for such openness in international commerce.